DEADLY DISEASES AND EPIDEMICS

CHOLERA

Second Edition

Antibiotic-resistant
  Bacteria

Anthrax, Second Edition

Avian Flu

Botulism

Campylobacteriosis

Cervical Cancer

Cholera, Second Edition

Dengue Fever and
  Other Hemorrhagic
  Viruses

Ebola

Encephalitis

Escherichia coli
  Infections

Gonorrhea

Hantavirus Pulmonary
  Syndrome

Helicobacter pylori

Hepatitis

Herpes

HIV/AIDS

Infectious Diseases of
  the Mouth

Infectious Fungi

Influenza,
  Second Edition

Legionnaires' Disease

Leprosy

Lung Cancer

Lyme Disease

Mad Cow Disease
  (Bovine Spongiform
  Encephalopathy)

Malaria

Meningitis

Mononucleosis,
  Second Edition

Pelvic Inflammatory
  Disease

Plague

Polio

Prostate Cancer

Rabies

Rocky Mountain
  Spotted Fever

Salmonella

SARS

Smallpox

Staphylococcus aureus
  Infections

Streptococcus (Group A)

Streptococcus (Group B)

Syphilis

Tetanus

Toxic Shock Syndrome

Trypanosomiasis

Tuberculosis

Tularemia

Typhoid Fever

West Nile Virus

DEADLY DISEASES AND EPIDEMICS

CHOLERA

Second Edition

William Coleman, Ph.D.

CONSULTING EDITOR
Hilary Babcock, M.D., M.P.H.,
Infectious Diseases Division,
Washington University School of Medicine,
Medical Director of Occupational Health (Infectious Diseases),
Barnes-Jewish Hospital and St. Louis Children's Hospital

FOREWORD BY
David Heymann
World Health Organization

CHELSEA HOUSE
P U B L I S H E R S
An imprint of Infobase Publishing

Deadly Diseases and Epidemics: Cholera, Second Edition

Copyright © 2009 by Infobase Publishing

Chelsea House
An imprint of Infobase Publishing
132 West 31st Street
New York, NY 10001

Library of Congress Cataloging-in-Publication Data
Coleman, William, 1937-
  Cholera / William Coleman ; consulting editor, Hilary Babcock ; foreword by David Heymann.
     p. cm. -- (Deadly diseases and epidemics)
  Includes bibliographical references and index.
  ISBN-13: 978-1-60413-232-8 (alk. paper)
  ISBN-10: 1-60413-232-9 (alk. paper)
  1. Cholera--Juvenile literature. I. Babcock, Hilary. II. Title. III. Series.

  RC126.C695 2008
  616.9'32--dc22

                              2008028627

Series design by Terry Mallon
Cover design by Takeshi Takahashi

Printed in the United States of America

Bang EJB 10 9 8 7 6 5 4 3 2 1

This book is printed on acid-free paper.

Table of Contents

Foreword
David Heymann, World Health Organization   6

1. Discovering Cholera   8

2. Properties of *Vibrio cholerae*   20

3. Dr. Snow and Cholera   33

4. Transmission and Epidemiology of Cholera   44

5. Signs and Symptoms of Cholera   57

6. The Virulence of *Vibrio cholerae*   67

7. The Genome of *Vibrio cholerae*   77

8. Treatments for Cholera   89

9. Prevention   100

10. Cholera Today   112

Notes   120

Glossary   123

Bibliography   130

Further Resources   134

Index   136

About the Author   142

About the Consulting Editor   142

Foreword

Communicable diseases kill and cause long-term disability. The microbial agents that cause them are dynamic, changeable, and resilient: they are responsible for more than 14 million deaths each year, mainly in developing countries.

Approximately 46 percent of all deaths in the developing world are due to communicable diseases, and almost 90 percent of these deaths are from AIDS, tuberculosis, malaria, and acute diarrheal and respiratory infections of children. In addition to causing great human suffering, these high-mortality communicable diseases have become major obstacles to economic development. They are a challenge to control either because of the lack of effective vaccines, or because the drugs that are used to treat them are becoming less effective because of antimicrobial drug resistance.

Millions of people, especially those who are poor and living in developing countries, are also at risk from disabling communicable diseases such as polio, leprosy, lymphatic filariasis, and onchocerciasis. In addition to human suffering and permanent disability, these communicable diseases create an economic burden—both on the work force that handicapped persons are unable to join, and on their families and society, upon which they must often depend for economic support.

Finally, the entire world is at risk of the unexpected communicable diseases, those that are called emerging or re-emerging infections. Infection is often unpredictable because risk factors for transmission are not understood, or because it often results from organisms that cross the species barrier from animals to humans. The cause is often viral, such as Ebola and Marburg hemorrhagic fevers and severe acute respiratory syndrome (SARS). In addition to causing human suffering and death, these infections place health workers at great risk and are costly to economies. Infections such as Bovine Spongiform Encephalopathy (BSE) and the associated new human variant of Creutzfeldt-Jakob Disease (vCJD) in Europe, and avian influenza A (H5N1) in Asia, are reminders of the seriousness of emerging and re-emerging infections. In addition, many of these infections have the potential to cause pandemics, which are a constant threat our economies and public health security.

Science has given us vaccines and anti-infective drugs that have helped keep infectious diseases under control. Nothing demonstrates the effectiveness of vaccines better than the successful eradication of smallpox, the decrease in polio as the eradication program continues, and the decrease in measles when routine immunization programs are supplemented by mass vaccination campaigns.

Likewise, the effectiveness of anti-infective drugs is clearly demonstrated through prolonged life or better health in those infected with viral diseases such as AIDS, parasitic infections such as malaria, and bacterial infections such as tuberculosis and pneumococcal pneumonia.

But current research and development is not filling the pipeline for new anti-infective drugs as rapidly as resistance is developing, nor is vaccine development providing vaccines for some of the most common and lethal communicable diseases. At the same time providing people with access to existing anti-infective drugs, vaccines, and goods such as condoms or bed nets—necessary for the control of communicable diseases in many developing countries—remains a great challenge.

Education, experimentation, and the discoveries that grow from them, are the tools needed to combat high mortality infectious diseases, diseases that cause disability, or emerging and re-emerging infectious diseases. At the same time, partnerships between developing and industrialized countries can overcome many of the challenges of access to goods and technologies. This book may inspire its readers to set out on the path of drug and vaccine development, or on the path to discovering better public health technologies by applying our present understanding of the human genome and those of various infectious agents. Readers may likewise be inspired to help ensure wider access to those protective goods and technologies. Such inspiration, with pragmatic action, will keep us on the winning side of the struggle against communicable diseases.

David L. Heymann
Assistant Director General,
Health Security and Environment
Representative of the Director General for Polio Eradication
World Health Organization
Geneva, Switzerland

1
Discovering Cholera

Refugee families were forced to flee Rwanda in the spring of 1997. Keren Mugabe, aged 12, left her home with her parents and two brothers. They went on foot, carrying what possessions they could, to the Republic of Congo.

Soon after her arrival in the Republic of Congo, Keren developed intense diarrhea. Constantly thirsty, her arm bones began to show through her skin. The nearest medical facility was nearly 15 miles away, but her father was able to find a ride with a Rwandan health care worker. At the health care facility, Keren saw many other refuges in similar states as she. Some were much worse off. At least she was not vomiting and had no fever. She was given fluids to drink. Unlike many other patients, she did not have to receive fluids by injection.

In a few days she began to feel better. She felt so sorry for the others at the camp who became more and more sick in spite of treatments. Keren felt lucky to have survived cholera.

What is cholera? "Cholera" is the term used to describe a specific gastrointestinal disease as well as the bacterium that causes that disease. In this case, the disease was known long before the **microorganism** that causes it was even recognized. To understand this, it is necessary to go back through history.

HEALTH IN VICTORIAN ENGLAND: MIASMA OR CONTAGION?

In the Victorian era (1837–1901) large cities often experienced outbreaks of diseases, including cholera. It is challenging today to picture the kinds of conditions that existed in the nineteenth century, particularly in large cities such as London. There was no safe sewage removal. As populations grew, waste removal systems proved inadequate. Bacteria normally recycle waste, but as city populations grew rapidly the volume of waste entering city sewers often overwhelmed this process. Methane gas formed by bacteria decomposing organic waste matter would accumulate and often explode!

These sewage fumes were called **miasmas**. Miasmas are the invisible emanations of toxic or harmful materials that arise from such things as swamps, garbage, and decaying matter. In the Victorian era some people believed that diseases such as cholera were spread in the toxic atmosphere from which miasmas arose. People who supported the miasma theory also believed that disease could be prevented by avoiding contact with miasmas.

Some public officials and physicians had other theories to explain the causes of cholera and other disease outbreaks. One of these was the **contagion** theory, which proposed that cholera was passed from person to person. Today, the ease with which an infections disease can be spread from person to person describes just how contagious the infectious disease may be. Some infectious agents are very contagious (influenza, for example), while others are less so (leprosy). This description does not consider the severity, toxicity, or type of infection. Rather, it describes the ease with which the infection can spread through a population.

Those who supported contagion theory thought that cholera was spread from person to person; however, they had no understanding of what was being passed from one person to another or how it was passed. Those who adhered to this contagion theory did not yet know that water contaminated with feces containing cholera bacteria might be a source of the contagion.

About the time of the London cholera outbreak of 1848–1849, a young physician named Dr. John Snow (1813–1858) became interested in cholera, both in developing a treatment as well as in pinpointing its source. He observed the case of John Harnold, a sailor who died from cholera in a rooming house in a part of London called Horsleydown. There had been no cases of cholera in this region for some time. However, the sailor had just arrived from Hamburg, Germany, where there had recently been an outbreak of cholera. A few days after this sailor died, another man stayed in the room Harnold had occupied. This man also got cholera, and the disease soon spread from Horsleydown to other neighborhoods. Eventually it spread throughout England.[1]

Dr. Snow realized that the series of events that led up to this cholera outbreak could not be explained by the miasma theory. Why would a room free of miasma suddenly contain toxic air after being free of it for some time?

There also remained mysteries that could not be explained by the contagion theory. Why did the doctor who attended both of the sick men remain healthy? This doctor had been in close contact with both men. More puzzlingly, why did cases of cholera begin to appear in the neighborhood of the boarding house in persons who had no contact with these men? Clearly, Dr. Snow could see that neither a miasma theory nor a contagion theory alone could explain the source of this disease. He began to collect records of cholera cases in an effort to uncover how cholera spread and how it could be prevented.

FLORENCE NIGHTINGALE

Around the same time as Dr. Snow began proposing new ideas about the cause and control of cholera, others held fast to different theories. One of the most famous adherents to the miasma theory was Florence Nightingale (1820–1910), a pioneer in the field of nursing. Nightingale is a much-revered figure who was responsible for many important reforms in the nursing profession and for invaluable improvements in nursing care. She believed that the air in rooms should be given an "air test" to ensure that organic material was removed. She recommended fresh air as long as patients were not chilled. Of course there is nothing wrong with this recommendation, but Nightingale did so in belief that all diseases were carried by air.

Figure 1.1   Florence Nightingale. (© U.S. National Institutes of Health/National Library of Medicine)

At a time when it was rare for women to travel alone, Florence Nightingale treated soldiers at the battlefront during the Crimean War. She was shocked at the poor sanitary conditions and health care given to the wounded soldiers. By changing these conditions, she became a pioneer in disease treatment and improved nursing.

Although improvements in health care emerged in the late 1800s, many important and well-motivated people such as Florence Nightingale still adhered to the idea that diseases were carried by miasmas. Without an understanding of the cause of infection and disease, surgeons unwittingly doomed their patients to death as soon as they began to operate. Surgeons did not think that there was a reason for cleanliness and touched their patients with unwashed hands and operated on them with dirty instruments. Most amputation patients died of infections resulting from surgery rather than from the initial wound. It was not yet known how to prevent the high rate of post-surgery deaths.

JOSEPH LISTER

High rates of surgical mortality began to change in part as a result of the efforts of the English physician Joseph Lister (1827–1912). In the 1850s Lister began his attempts to reduce infections in hospitals, particularly as a result of surgery, by using carbolic acid (phenol) to cleanse rooms, surgical instruments, and wounds. It took him more than 25 years before these efforts were appreciated. In 1877 he showed that the uses of his methods for cleansing in hospitals had reduced mortality by 50 percent.

At the same time that Dr. Lister was developing methods for preventing infections, others were investigating the causes of infection and disease. Two of Lister's contemporaries, Louis Pasteur and Robert Koch, made important discoveries that would soon change the way medicine was practiced.

Figure 1.2   Joseph Lister. (© U.S. National Institutes of Health/National Library of Medicine)

THE GERM THEORY OF DISEASE

Microorganisms were not widely recognized as the causes of many diseases until late in the nineteenth century. However, some early scientists did propose that living organisms caused illnesses. The Italian physician Girolamo Fracastoro (ca. 1478–1553) spoke of "seeds" or "germs" of disease. Translations of Fracastoro's Latin writings indicate that he may have surmised that these "seeds" were alive. This is the earliest known written record of the **germ theory of disease**, the concept that microorganisms cause some diseases. This concept was neglected for many years, however.

LOUIS PASTEUR AND ROBERT KOCH

In the mid-nineteenth century the famous French scientist Louis Pasteur (1822–1895) had proven that microorganisms do not arise spontaneously. His classic, simplistic, and ingenious experiment was to design a flask with an S-shaped curve in its neck. The curve trapped microorganisms that were present in the air before they could reach the main part of the flask. He filled flasks with broth, heated them, and then allowed them to cool. In previous experiments using flasks without the S-shaped neck, microorganisms would grow in the broth. This did not occur in Pasteur's experiments. Critics stated that a "vital force" had been removed from the air by heating, so the microorganisms could not grow. Pasteur's flasks allowed the air to have access to the heated broth, defusing this argument. His cooled flasks did not become spoiled with bacterial growth because the microorganisms in the air had no means to ascend the tube leading to the broth once they were trapped in the dip, or curve, of the S-shaped flask. Pasteur went on to show that when he broke the spout of the flask, thereby destroying the S-shaped spout with the dip in it, the bacteria present in the air quickly grew in the broth. This experiment established once and for all that microorganisms do not arise spontaneously.

In addition to this landmark experiment, Pasteur went on to make numerous contributions to understanding microorganisms and how they affected animals. Pasteur, along with his main competitor, the German scientist Robert Koch

Figure 1.3 Robert Koch discovered that certain microorganisms can cause specific diseases. Along with studying anthrax and cholera, his rules for proving that a microorganism causes disease has become the standard practice of microbiology today. These rules are known as Koch's Postulates. (© Bettmann/ Corbis)

(1843–1910), studied numerous microorganisms and the effects they caused, including diseases.

Robert Koch was the first person to show that a specific microbe can cause an infectious disease in a higher animal. He isolated the bacterium that causes tuberculosis in 1882. A year later, he published a report describing the bacterium that causes the disease cholera. This microorganism is called *Vibrio cholerae*. How was Koch able to isolate this one microorganism and associate it with cases of the infection?

In order to isolate and identify *Vibrio cholerae*, Koch had to grow this microorganism free from all other microorganisms. A microorganism grown in this manner is called a **pure culture** of a microorganism. In addition, Koch had to develop a growth **medium**, as well as a technique to separate the many thousands of microbes in a sample so that just one microbe could grow, dividing repeatedly to form visible growth. This growth is referred to as a **colony** of a specific bacterium.

KOCH'S TECHNIQUES
FOR THE STUDY OF MICROBES

Koch first made a growth medium using 2.5 to 5 percent gelatin (a protein obtained from the tendons of animals) in a nutrient soup. He spread the medium on a glass slide and allowed it to solidify at room temperature. Next, he sterilized a metal wire by heating it in a flame. When the wire cooled, Koch dipped it into the area where the bacteria were located, and used the wire to draw a line onto the solid medium on the slide. He repeated this process many times, as illustrated in Figure 1.4.

Koch then placed the slide in a warm incubator. After the bacteria had grown on the medium, the slide was removed for observation. The first streaks on the slide contained many microbes. Each subsequent streak had fewer microbes. Eventually, only single cells grew in each area. After the cells had been allowed to grow overnight, the single cells had formed colonies about .039–.078 inches (1–2 mm) in diameter. Colonies are

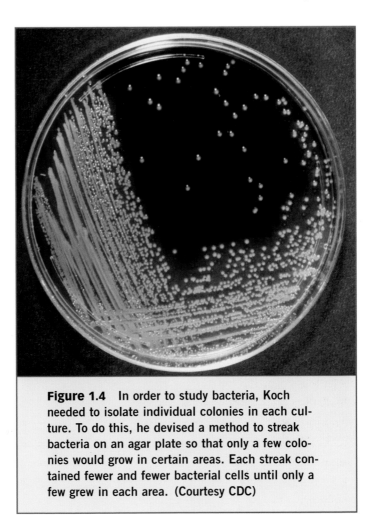

Figure 1.4 In order to study bacteria, Koch needed to isolate individual colonies in each culture. To do this, he devised a method to streak bacteria on an agar plate so that only a few colonies would grow in certain areas. Each streak contained fewer and fewer bacterial cells until only a few grew in each area. (Courtesy CDC)

individual microbes that have divided repeatedly to form a group of cells visible to the naked eye. Each colony was a **clone**, a pure culture of identical cells.

Koch had problems with the use of gelatin in this procedure. Many microorganisms could degrade the gelatin protein, turning the medium to mush. In addition, gelatin melts at body temperature, the very temperature that is most likely to support the growth of an infectious microorganism. A turn of events, which

is by now a legend, occurred. The wife of one of Koch's cowork-
ers suggested using a cooking additive for the growth medium
instead of gelatin. The additive was called **agar**. She had learned
from a Dutch friend that this substance was often used in preparing jellies and soups in Java, a former Dutch colony and now part
of Indonesia. Agar is dried seaweed that can be ground and dissolved when heated in water. It remains in a liquid form for some
hours at 122°F (50°C), and it solidifies below 107.6°F (42°C).
Koch recognized that agar provided a better growth medium than
gelatin for the isolation of pure cultures. It remains in use today.

Another legacy of Koch's early lab is the glass dish that was
developed by an assistant of Koch, R. J. Petri. The petri dish

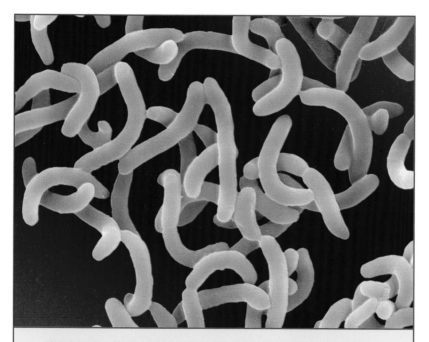

Figure 1.5 This electron micrograph shows the curved and
spiral nature of the *Vibrio* bacteria. Koch found that older
cultures contained more spiral-shaped vibrios, while newer cultures contained more comma-shaped bacteria. (© Dr. Dennis
Kunkel/Visuals Unlimited)

is standard today in the study of microorganisms. One can see colonies without removing the cover of the dish. The agar medium can be varied while it is still liquid, then poured into petri dishes rather than spread onto glass slides, as Koch had done originally.

The **streak plate method** for the isolation of pure cultures of bacteria is also standard today. These methods had to be developed before Koch could establish that microorganisms caused cholera and other diseases. When he first observed the microbes he isolated, they appeared as small commas, so he referred to them as "comma bacilli." Another name for this curved rod-shaped type of bacteria is a vibrio. Hence, the official name for this microorganism is *Vibrio cholerae*.

KOCH'S POSTULATES

Not content merely to observe a microbe present in an infected individual, Koch established guidelines for proving that a microbe causes a particular infection. These guidelines are called Koch's Postulates and are still used today as standards for establishing proof of infection. They are, in brief:

1. The microbe has to be present in every case of the disease.

2. The microbe has to be isolated from the patient and grown in pure culture.

3. When the purified microorganism is inoculated into a healthy susceptible host, the same disease results.

4. Once again, the same microbe must be isolated from the host infected with the microbe.

Koch's remarkable contributions were landmarks in the fields of microbiology, medicine, and scientific study in general. He received the Nobel Prize in Medicine in 1905 for his work related to tuberculosis; moreover, his techniques and protocols for laboratory investigation are still in use today.

2

Properties of
Vibrio cholerae

Koch discovered that *Vibrio cholerae* causes cholera. But how is this organism unique? Does it resemble other microorganisms that cause similar diseases? How is it different? How can this information help distinguish *Vibrio cholerae* from the thousands of other microorganisms that inhabit the human body at any given time?

KOCH'S FIRST LOOK

In 1883, Koch headed a commission established by the German government to study cholera in Egypt and India. His discovery of the comma bacilli in a large number of cases of the disease indicated that a bacillus of this same shape was probably present every time. In addition, Koch was able to see firsthand the transmission of the disease and subsequent infection by the bacilli when two of his laboratory assistants became seriously ill and nearly died after drinking cholera-tainted water.

What Koch saw in his study of *Vibrio cholerae* was a small, curved rod, ranging in length from one to two microns, which is only one or two millionths of a meter. The microbes curved in various ways: Some were only slightly bent while others had spirals of one or two turns that looked like corkscrews. The bacterium was also actively **motile**. When Koch stained the bacteria with a special stain, he could see that each organism contained a single polar flagellum, or tail. The organisms did not appear to form **spores**. Young cultures contained more comma-shaped

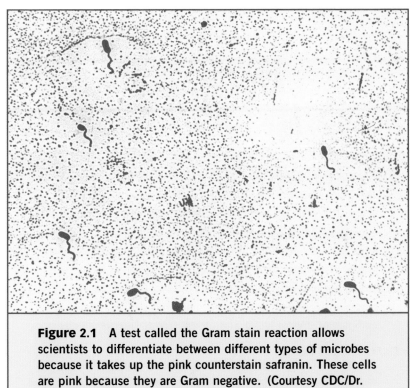

Figure 2.1   A test called the Gram stain reaction allows scientists to differentiate between different types of microbes because it takes up the pink counterstain safranin. These cells are pink because they are Gram negative. (Courtesy CDC/Dr. William A. Clark)

forms while the spiral forms of the microbe dominated older cultures. It is now known that if the microbe is grown in the laboratory and does not pass through an animal body, the microbes tend to lose their curvature entirely. Koch also observed that the microorganism was decolorized when using the **Gram stain reaction.**

LOOKING AT THE CHOLERA BACILLUS TODAY

Today, *Vibrio cholerae* is classified as Gram negative, since it decolorizes after staining with crystal violet but takes up the **counterstain** safranin (Figure 2.1).

The cholera bacillus is fairly easy to grow in the laboratory. It will grow in most common laboratory media such as nutrient broth or nutrient agar but will also grow on meat extracts. The organism prefers media that is moderately alkaline, but this is not essential since it will also tolerate mild acidity. Small, strongly refracting yellowish-gray colonies appear after 24 hours

THE GRAM STAIN REACTION

The Gram stain was developed in 1884 by Hans Christian Gram. This staining procedure differentiates bacteria into two categories, Gram positive and Gram negative. First, the microorganisms are attached to a glass slide and then stained with crystal violet dye. An iodine solution consisting of iodine and iodide ion is then applied to the bacteria. The crystal violet reacts with the iodine solution inside the bacterial cells. A complex of crystal violet and iodine forms. Next, the cells are treated with 95 percent ethyl alcohol solution. Some cells will retain the purple color after the alcohol treatment and are designated as Gram positive bacteria. Other cells will lose the purple color of the dye (the crystal violet-iodine complex washes out) and are considered Gram negative. Gram negative bacteria are then stained with safranin, which gives them a contrasting light red color. Cholera bacilli are Gram negative.

Years later, it was discovered that there are fundamental structural differences between Gram negative and Gram positive bacteria. Gram positive bacteria have a thick cell wall surrounding the cell membrane. Gram negative bacteria have a cell membrane, a thin cell wall over that, and an additional lipid bilayer membrane outside the cell wall and facing the exterior of the cell. This additional lipid bilayer contains components that are unique for each species of Gram negative bacteria.

Gram positive and Gram negative bacteria have different properties and characteristics because of these distinctly different cell structures.

of growth on gelatin plates. However, the gelatin liquifies as the organism continues to grow. The colonies are coarsely granular with uneven edges due to the liquefaction of the gelatin. In gelatin stab cultures, liquefaction begins at the top, leading to a funnel-shaped pattern of gelatin liquifaction. This ability to attack gelatin is lost in old strains of the bacterium that have been grown artificially in the laboratory for long periods.

On agar plates, grayish and opalescent colonies appear within 18 to 24 hours. The fact that *Vibrio cholerae* is opalescent helps in the identification and isolation of these microorganisms from patients because other bacteria likely to appear in feces are not opalescent. In addition, the bacillus can liquify coagulated blood serum and can also grow on starch, appearing as a brownish coarse growth. The cholera bacillus grows abundantly on alkaline peptone medium. This trait is particularly helpful when a scientist needs to isolate the microorganism from mixed samples, such as a fecal specimen. The cholera bacillus also produces a crystalline compound called indole, which also helps with identification.

Vibrio species can grow at a broad temperature range in the lab (from 64°F to 98.6°F or 18°C to 37°C) on a variety of simple media, aerobically or anaerobically. Therefore, the bacterium is described as **aerobic** and facultatively anaerobic. It grows optimally at 99.5°F (37.5°C), which is normal human body temperature. The microorganism has a positive oxidase reaction, which means that is has the enzyme cytochrome oxidase, a key enzyme in aerobic metabolism.

Cholera bacteria can live about three or four days when frozen in ice. They die immediately when heated to boiling (212°F, or 100°C). They are killed within an hour at a temperature of 140°F, or 60°C. Drying will also kill the cells in a short period of time. Dilute solutions of common disinfectants destroy these bacteria after exposure for a few minutes. When in impure water, in food, on cloth, or other complex environmental conditions, they may live for many days, allowing more people to become infected from contaminated water supplies.

ISOLATING CHOLERA BACILLI FROM PATIENTS

The properties of *Vibrio cholerae* discussed in the previous section are important for the isolation and identification of cholera bacilli from patient specimens. The procedures for examination of **stool specimens** from patients outline methods to test for: 1) animal parasites, 2) routine examinations for microorganisms, and finally 3) examinations for special or unusual cases. The search for cholera bacilli falls into this third category, since it is not an ordinary or suspected disease in the United States. However, in areas where cholera is more commonly observed, the procedures for isolating and identifying cholera bacilli are undoubtedly routine. If a virus is suspected, **tissue culture** and electron microscopy methods are also used in an attempt to identify the offending microorganism. Sample specimens from special cases are placed in culture medium at 71.6°F (22°C), inoculated into alkaline peptone water, which will help to increase the number of bacilli in the sample, and streaked on thiosulfate-citrate-bile salt-sucrose (TCBS) medium plates. TCBS plates also contain a bromothymol blue indicator that helps to identify colonies. Microorganisms that do not ferment sucrose grow best on TCBS medium and produce blue-green colonies. Because *Vibrio cholerae* does ferment sucrose, it will produce yellow-colored colonies on this medium. The fermentation process involves the formation of acid from sucrose, and the acid reacts with bromothymol blue, resulting in a color change. The **bile salts** in this medium and the high pH (8.6) prevent the growth of other bacteria associated with the gastrointestinal tract. Cholera bacilli in fresh stool samples will also have a characteristic darting mobility, which aids in the identification of the microorganism.

In addition to flagella, there are shorter, smaller appendages on these bacteria called fimbriae and pili. These two terms are often used interchangeably. Fimbriae are thin fibrils commonly found in many bacteria. Pili are the fimbria found in many intestinal bacteria such as *Vibrio cholerae*. Pili are important for bacterial attachment to viruses, to host cells, and to other bacteria during mating.

Having proceeded this far, one might think that the search for cholera bacilli in a patient sample is complete. This is true, yet it is still necessary to identify what type of strain is present, as many different strains of the bacillus exist. The strains can be identified by matching them to antibodies that are formed against each different type. In order to understand this process, one must examine the structural variations that define each of the strains.

THE CHOLERA BACILLUS AS A PROKARYOTE OF THE DOMAIN BACTERIA

All life forms are either **prokaryotes** or **eukaryotes**. Eukaryotic cells contain a nucleus and other membrane-bound organelles. The DNA of the eukaryotic cell is contained on chromosomes that are located within the nucleus. Animal, plant, and fungal cells are eukaryotes. Prokaryotes, on the other hand, are generally smaller in size and do not have a nucleus or membrane-bound organelles, and the DNA resides within the cytoplasm. Bacteria are prokaryotes.

There are three distinct types of life forms on Earth. Two of these categories, Archaea and Bacteria, are prokaryotes. Organisms in the Archaea group are thought to be the oldest life forms that still exist on Earth. These microorganisms live in extreme places in our environment such as regions of high salt and high temperature, and places where methane can be formed. For this reason, Archaea microorganisms are often referred to as extremophiles. For example, the hot geyser pools in Yellowstone National Park, Wyoming, have yielded numerous high temperature–growing microorganisms called thermophiles. Microorganisms in the group Archaea differ from those in the group Bacteria in several ways. Archaea have a different cell wall composition than Bacteria. Scientists have discovered that *Vibrio* organisms are part of the domain Bacteria.

Bacteria are usually categorized as Gram positive or Gram negative. The Gram stain procedure utilizes a primary stain, crystal violet, and a secondary stain, safranin. Cells are first treated with crystal violet, and then rinsed. Next, safranin is added. Cells that are considered Gram positive will retain the crystal violet dye even after they are rinsed. Gram negative cells will not retain the primary stain. Recall that Koch and others determined that *Vibrio cholerae* was Gram negative. Nearly 50 years later, scientists discovered that chemical differences in the cell walls of different cells leads to the distinction in staining characteristics.

Gram negative bacteria have an outer as well as an inner cell membrane layer. Both the outer and inner cell membranes are composed of lipid bilayers. However, the additional lipid bilayer in Gram negative bacteria necessitates the formation of protein structures called **porins**, which help transport water-soluble materials into the bacterial cell. This is why these bacteria do not retain the crystal violet dye. In contrast, Gram positive microorganisms have a thick layer of cell wall polymer above the single lipid bilayer cell membrane, which causes the bacteria to retain the crystal violet dye.

The outer membrane of a Gram negative bacterial cell contains numerous proteins and lipopolysaccharides. Each element has an important function. **Lipid A** is attached to the outermost layer of the membrane. A core polysaccharide is attached to Lipid A. Each core polysaccharide has a special side chain that varies from one species of Gram negative bacteria to another. This entire complex, the core polysaccharide and the side chain, is called a lipopolysaccharide (**LPS**). The LPS plus Lipid A is called an **endotoxin** because the complex is toxic to many different animals.

ANTIBODIES AS A RESPONSE TO THE
OUTER STRUCTURES OF CHOLERA BACILLI

Like nearly all foreign invaders, the cholera bacilli will invoke an immune response from its host. Any substance that invokes an immune response is called an **antigen** and alerts the host organism to form antibodies. An **antibody** is a protein that attacks a specific foreign substance or antigen. Early investigations by German microbiologists recognized two major types of antibodies that formed in response to bacteria like the cholera bacillus. One type of antibody could recognize the proteins of the flagella. The Germans used their word for "film" (*Hauch*) to describe these antibodies. These microbes can move, and they were observed to form films across the surfaces of media. These became known as H antigens or flagellar antigens. The antibodies that formed against the rest of the cell were said to be "without film" (*ohne Hauch*) and thus were designated O antigens. These are also referred to as somatic or cellular antigens, indicating that these are part of the main body or structure of the bacterial cells. The polar flagellum and fimbria of *Vibrio cholerae* can be seen using an electron microscope.

Scientists have discovered about 150 different strains of *Vibrio cholerae*. Cholera outbreaks have been predominantly caused by the O1 serogroup of *Vibrio cholerae*. This **serogroup** contains two **biotypes**: the classical and the more recently recognized *El Tor*. The *El Tor* strain was isolated from the pilgrims at El Tor on Egypt's Sinai Peninsula in 1905. The *El Tor* biotype is usually associated with a milder disease and a higher rate of asymptomatic **carriers**. Each biotype, classical and *El Tor*, contains different serotypes: *Ogawa, Inaba*, and *Hikojima*, distinguished by different immunological reactions. In 1992, a new **serotype**, designated *O139 syn. Bengal*, was isolated in Bangaladesh.[1]

There are three different polysaccharides that have been found as part of the O1 antigen structure. These are indicated as types A, B, and C. These polysaccharides help to further

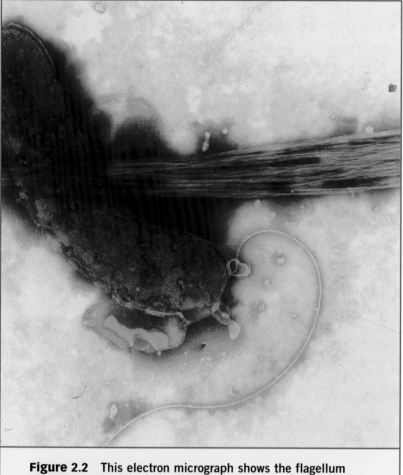

Figure 2.2 This electron micrograph shows the flagellum and fimbria of a *Vibrio cholerae* bacterium. The flagellum is a tail-like projection that helps the cell to move. (Courtesy Dartmouth College Rippel Electron Microscope Facility)

differentiate cholera strains. The Ogawa strain has types A and B, the Inaba strain has types A and C, and a rare type has been found that has all three of these polysaccharides (Hikojima strain). They can be distinguished by using antibodies specific to each strain and by comparing reactions to the different bacterial strains. For example, antibodies to the Ogawa strain would react best when mixed with antibodies to the Ogawa bacillus. However, there would be some reaction with the Inaba strain, since it shares the A polysaccharide in the O1 antigen. The reaction of antigens and antibodies is usually observed by mixing antigens and antibodies on slides and observing agglutination (clumping) due to the large antigen-antibody complexes that form and precipitate from solution.

Now, the identification of the cholera bacillus is complete. Performing **slide agglutination** tests on the microbes isolated from the stool specimen by growth on TCBS agar can indicate the specific serotype found. This is particularly important for tracking a specific type of cholera bacillus during epidemics.

However, one can not assume that all strains of *Vibrio cholerae* have been discovered. It is possible that new strains can form if current forms of the organism mutate. Should that happen, there are methods to identify, characterize, and hopefully develop appropriate treatments for the new strains. One of these newer methods of identification involves the use of bacterial viruses, called bacteriophages.

BACTERIOPHAGES OF VIBRIO CHOLERAE

Viruses that attack bacteria, **bacteriophages**, have been identified for *Vibrio cholerae.* These bacteriophages (or phages, for short) are either **temperate** or **virulent**. Temperate phages can integrate their genetic material into a bacterial host. When this integration occurs, the host bacterium has obtained new DNA from the infecting virus that can be passed down during multiplication. This process is called **lysogeny**, and the temperate phage is said to be lysogenic. Virulent phages do not integrate their genetic material into the host bacteria they attack. Usually, virulent phages kill their host cells by causing them to lyse, or burst. This is called a lytic infection.

On rare occasions, lysogenic cells can be treated such that the viral genome is removed from the host cell, and the entire virus reproduces in it, initiating a lysis cycle. Viruses described for *Vibrio cholerae* are both temperate and lytic. Lytic phages are found more frequently in El Tor *Vibrio* strains, but are not found as often in classical *Vibrio* strains.

Vibriophages—bacterial viruses that attack *Vibrio* species—have been isolated that are temperate and capable of introducing their DNA at random sites in the host genome; this introduces disruptions in host genes and causes the formation of mutant bacterial cells when these cells reproduce. Discovering vibriophages has given scientists tools to understand distinct ways that bacteria can transmit DNA through a bacterial population. That, in turn, helps understanding of the sources of various pathogenic strains of bacteria as well as the rise of antibiotic resistance in certain bacteria. In addition, phages can be used in a new way to track various strains of bacteria by a method called **phage typing**.[2, 3]

TOXIC STRAINS ARE LYSOGENIC

Lysogeny can result in measurable changes in the chemistry and structure of a host bacterial cell because that cell harbors new genetic material from the temperate phage. These changes are called phage conversion. After phage conversion, strains of *Vibrio cholerae* bacteria produce new factors that make them virulent, meaning that they now can cause symptomatic cholera. One of the factors is cholera toxin (CT), a potent enterotoxin that binds to the intestinal lining and causes leakage of water and chloride, resulting in diarrhea and dehydration. This is the toxin that triggers cholera's diarrhea symptom. CT is produced after the lysogenic filamentous phage CTX infects a strain of cholera bacteria.[4]

PHAGE TYPING

Bacteriophages can infect only bacteria that have receptors that they can bind to, which means that not every pairing of phage and bacteria is a "match" for infection. Phage typing is a technique to find the different bacteriophages that a bacterium is susceptible to. For example, a number of different virulent bacteriophages are first isolated from a strain of *Vibrio cholerae*. They are purified and stored. When a new outbreak occurs, that bacterial strain is isolated, purified, and grown over an entire plate containing growth medium. Usually a grid is drawn on the underside of the plate, and using this as a guide, drops of each of the purified phages are placed on the bacteria. After incubating, the plates are examined for zones of clearing. If there is a zone of clearing from a particular phage, the investigator knows that this particular strain is susceptible to this phage. Identical bacterial strains will have identical profiles of phages that can attack successfully. This can be used to trace the origins of a particular outbreak as well as the extent of its spread during an outbreak.

HORIZONTAL VERSUS VERTICAL TRANSMISSION OF GENETIC MATERIAL

When DNA is replicated, the genetic information it contains is copied and transferred to the new daughter cells during cell division. This type of mechanism for transfer of genetic information in a population is called vertical transmission. Bacteria have another means of sharing genetic information, however. The DNA from outside sources such as viruses and other bacteria can be used to introduce new DNA into and between bacterial cells, and this is not coupled with cell division. This means that a population can change very quickly to adapt to new environments. This transfer of genetic information from one population to another is called horizontal transmission. Introduction of new genetic material to a strain of cholera bacteria by a bacteriophage is an example.[5]

ANTIBIOTIC RESISTANCE

The earliest examples of horizontal gene transfer found were observations of antibiotic resistance. It was seen that bacteria could acquire antibiotic resistance genes at rates much higher than could be accounted for by normal mutation rates in populations alone. Upon closer examination, it was found that sections of DNA in the cytoplasm of antibiotic resistant bacteria can be passed horizontally to other nonresistant strains. This DNA is often located in the bacterial cell's cytoplasm as a free, circular DNA element that is not a part of the cell's chromosome, and it is called a **plasmid**.

The problem of antibiotic resistance remains a serious one for health professionals. Through horizontal transmission of resistance genes, resistance can spread quickly through a bacterial population. Infections caused by antibiotic resistant bacterial strains will not respond to commonly used antibiotics, resulting in prolonged and more severe illness and increased spread through a community. Treatment options become limited and disease control becomes more challenging.

3

Dr. Snow and Cholera

In 1831 in Newcastle-upon-Tyne, England, a group of coal miners who had been perfectly fit and healthy in the morning returned from a day working in the mines profusely **defecating** with abundant watery **diarrhea**. They were in a state of near exhaustion. Granted, their work in the mines was hard and the conditions grueling, but this could not explain the fact that soon most of the miners collapsed and died.

John Snow (Figure 3.1), then 18 years old and in his second year as apprentice to the local doctor at Newcastle-upon-Tyne, was sent to give the miners and their families any medical assistance that he could. Although Dr. Snow knew at once that the men were ill with cholera, there was little he could do for them. Cholera was familiar to the British from their visits to India, where it was common. The miners were exhibiting the same symptoms as people believed to be suffering from cholera in India.

After seven more years as an apprentice to several physicians, Snow passed the medical examinations. At the age of 25, he set up practice as a physician and sold drugs and other medicines. He could have continued to practice medicine with no further education or medical degrees. For him, though, his present knowledge about infectious diseases was not enough. Most physicians of the day believed that cholera and other such infectious diseases were carried through miasmas, or "bad air." Snow did not agree. Furthermore, he was intrigued by many unanswered questions in the medical field and thus decided to study medicine further. He attended the college and the newly opened medical school at the University of London when he was 30 years old and graduated in 1844.

Figure 3.1   John Snow discovered the path of cholera transmission through his careful observation of the 1854 cholera epidemic in London. He was the first scientist to propose that cholera was transmitted through contaminated water. (U.S. National Institutes of Health/National Library of Medicine)

SCIENTIFIC CURIOSITY

In addition to practicing medicine, Snow was interested in many topics in medicine, including lead poisoning, stillbirths, scarlet fever, smallpox, and blood vessels. He became interested in the use of ether in anesthesia in 1846, after he observed a dentist using the technique. Ether anesthesia had been introduced earlier that year by Dr. William Morton at Massachusetts General Hospital in Boston.

Snow observed that there was great variation in dosage and patient response to the ether. Some patients did not recover from the administration of ether. Snow realized that the dosage was very dependent on the temperature of the room. The higher the temperature, the greater the dosage needed. He published a table for calculating the amount of dosage at different temperatures. This was one of numerous publications and articles that Snow produced at this time.

His fame as a physician and anesthesiologist grew, and he was much sought after for his services. He administered ether anesthetic successfully to Queen Victoria in 1853. His intense curiosity and research efforts in many areas of medicine demonstrate a keen scientific mind.

INTEREST IN CHOLERA

No one is certain the precise moment that Snow became interested in cholera. Certainly the London cholera outbreak of 1848–1849, would have been of interest for the many questions it raised. Snow realized from the cases that arose at the Horsleydown rooming house that the cause of cholera could not be explained by either a miasma or contagion theory alone. In the case of the sailor John Harnold, Snow observed that a room previously free of cholera miasma suddenly had occupants, one after another, who came down with the disease. Further, the attending physician who entered the room and had direct contact with both patients did not get cholera via the contagion route. Finally, more cases of the disease suddenly appeared within the same neighborhood and proceeded to spread to the surrounding areas.

Snow was aware of documented cases of cholera in India that dated as far back as 1789. However, it is likely that cholera existed in India before Europeans went there for regular visits. As travel between India and Europe increased, it is very likely that cholera followed them home. Because the first cases of cholera in England were thought to have originated in India, the disease was often called Asiatic cholera.

DR. SNOW'S DATA COLLECTION

Snow knew of many cases in which it seemed clear that the disease was carried from a sick person to a healthy person. After observing cases like the sailor John Harnold, Snow began to collect information from many such cases. Many learned men of the day thought that diseases such as cholera were carried from one person to another through the air. Snow wanted to find out for sure. He began to collect information from many cases and kept careful records.

Many of his medical colleagues also kept records. From all his experiences, both in treating patients and in examinations after death, he observed that the main part of the body affected by cholera was the **alimentary canal**, the part of the body responsible for digestion. He began to think that cholera might be spread through drinking water. Snow believed that this was the method of disease **communication**.

Snow formed the **hypothesis** that cholera is a communicable disease spread through water. Following the scientific method for problem solving, he continued his clinical observations, carefully collecting data that might prove his preliminary idea. However, the many clinical cases in which cholera had passed to a healthy person from a person who had been in contact with an infected individual did not prove or disprove his hypothesis. In some of these cases, the persons who became ill were near to but not in contact with the patient at all. Yet, some got cholera and some did not. Why was this so?

One outbreak was particularly telling. Rows of small cottages were separated by a single street in Horsleydown, England. The north side of the cottages was called Surrey Buildings, and the south side of the cottages was called Truscott's Court. During 1849 there were many cases of cholera in the Surrey Buildings but only two cases in Truscott's Court. The two sets of buildings received their well water from different water companies. Household wastewater was poured into a channel in front of the houses in both cases; however, the wastewater from the residents of the Surrey Buildings reached the well that the residents used for drinking water. Truscott's Court's wastewater did not contaminate the well that the residents used.

Snow did not draw conclusions from any one case. Rather, he examined many cases and their extent, appearance, and geographical location before formulating any conclusions. In short, he was the first scientist to use methods of **epidemiology**, which are employed to this day.

DR. SNOW USES MAPS
TO HELP TRACK THE DISEASE

Outbreaks of cholera occurred regularly during the nineteenth century. In 1854, Snow reported one of the most severe outbreaks to date. In a period of three days, 127 people in the area of Broad Street in London died from the disease. Snow kept records of this **epidemic** by marking a street map of the area with the location of each of the cholera patients (Figures 3.2 and 3.3). He saw that there were more cases closer to the water pump, and the numbers of cases diminished at distances from the water pump. Sanitary conditions were similar in other areas of the neighborhood, but there were few or no cases of cholera in the vicinity of other water pumps. This convinced Snow that this cholera outbreak was the result of drinking water from the Broad Street water pump.

Snow also realized that some people who lived far from the city and Broad Street were dying of cholera even though they most likely did not use water from the Broad Street pump. In order to prove his theory that cholera was not "in the air," but in the water, he investigated one such case. A lady from Hampstead, a suburb of the city of London, had died of

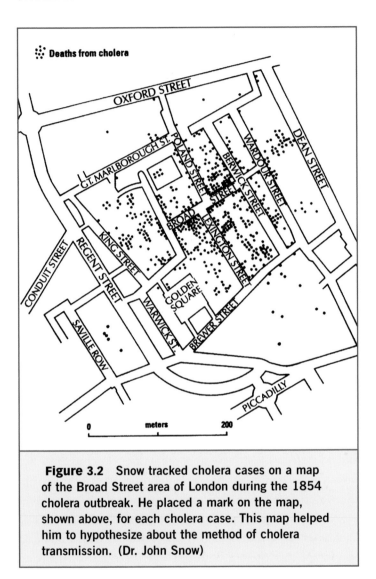

Deaths from cholera

Figure 3.2 Snow tracked cholera cases on a map of the Broad Street area of London during the 1854 cholera outbreak. He placed a mark on the map, shown above, for each cholera case. This map helped him to hypothesize about the method of cholera transmission. (Dr. John Snow)

cholera. Her son told Snow that she had not been in the vicinity of Broad Street for many months. This was truly puzzling. The water in the household was clear and had never been in contact with sewage. Snow began questioning members of the household, including the staff. One servant told him

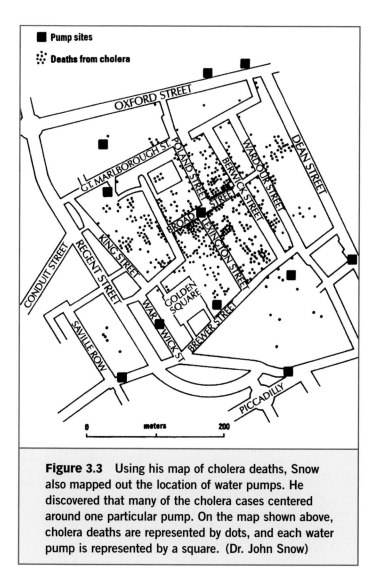

Pump sites

Deaths from cholera

Figure 3.3 Using his map of cholera deaths, Snow also mapped out the location of water pumps. He discovered that many of the cholera cases centered around one particular pump. On the map shown above, cholera deaths are represented by dots, and each water pump is represented by a square. (Dr. John Snow)

that the woman had had a fondness for water drawn from the pump at Broad Street in London. The servant was sent to the Broad Street neighborhood to draw water from the pump and had done so during the time of the cholera epidemic. The woman, in turn, drank this water. This was the connection that Snow was looking for. The mystery surrounding cholera **transmission** had been solved.

Snow also realized that there were fewer cases of cholera in the area just east of the Broad Street pump (see Figures 3.2 and 3.3). Snow talked to the owners of a brewery located in this area and found that the workers at the brewery did not drink from the Broad Street pump because the owner of the brewery supplied beer for his workers. He assured Snow that these men drank beer and not water! This helped explain the lower numbers of cholera cases in that area of the city.

Snow realized that something had to be done to reduce the transmission of cholera in the area. He discussed the problem with the Board of Guardians of St. James's Parish, which had jurisdiction over the area of the Broad Street water pump. Snow told them that the pump was the source of the cholera in this latest epidemic, and he recommended that they shut it down. Very reluctantly, they heeded his advice to do so, and the pump handle was removed.

Although this particular epidemic may have already reached its peak and was beginning to wane by the time Snow convinced St. James's Parish to remove the pump handle, it is certain that his research prevented future infections from the Broad Street water pump. In later years, this set of observations has been referred to as the "Grand Experiment" of Snow and has entered the realm of folklore in the history of medicine.

THE FATHER OF EPIDEMIOLOGY

Snow is hailed today as the founder of the science of epidemiology. This is justified when one appreciates his methods to study the spread of cholera. He had contemporaries who were interested in the studies of diseases in populations, however. One was Dr. Ignaz Semmelweis, who studied the incidence of childbirth fever at Austria's Vienna General Hospital in 1847. Semmelweis observed that most cases occurred after medical students had examined expectant mothers. The students had not washed their hands before treating the expectant mothers, and often had come to the ward right after performing autopsies. When the medical students were ordered to wash their hands before delivering babies, the rate of the infection dropped dramatically. Later in the century, Florence Nightingale kept data showing that unsanitary conditions, food quality, and diseases were responsible for deaths. Her studies led to reforms in the British army. Even without knowing the cause of infection, these pioneers used documented population studies to bring about reforms.

EPIDEMIOLOGY TODAY

Snow's method for studying a disease is just one approach used by modern epidemiologists. Snow's search for the cause of cholera is an example of a descriptive approach. A descriptive approach involves collecting all information describing the occurrence of a disease under study and looking for patterns. Snow's search for the cause of cholera is an example of this approach.

Today, even deeper analyses can be done. Analytical epidemiology can be done by a case control method. In this case the epidemiologist compares two groups, one with a disease and one without a disease. In this way, characteristics of the two groups can be compared to define risk factors for the disease. In a cohort method, one compares two groups—one with contact with a suspected disease agent and one without any contact—and determines who gets sick. For example, comparing those who have had blood transfusions with those who have not in a study of blood-borne pathogens. In experimental epidemiology, infected groups may be compared, some treated and some untreated. (If the treatment is a success, the untreated group is quickly given proper care.) In all of these approaches, computer technologies have enabled epidemiologists to compare many more factors in order to study and track epidemics.

Today, satellites are used to monitor climate, temperature, precipitation, and vegetation changes in order to predict continental and global patterns of disease outbreaks. The field of landscape epidemiology is the study of patterns of disease transmission relating these factors in geographic landscapes. Such factors as vegetation, water content, and geology of a landscape are related to the distribution, spread, and transmission of infectious diseases. Included in this technology are remote sensors for light, radiation, and object images at high resolution. Then a computer-based geographical information system (GIS) is used for analysis of the large amounts of data.[1]

Snow used maps to locate cases of cholera over 150 years ago. Today, sophisticated GIS systems provide digital maps as well as other information. A GIS application is a hybrid of maps, graphs, and databases that can display and interpret multiple dimensions of information.[2, 3, 4, 5]

TRACKING EPIDEMICS

Did you know that satellites can track worldwide epidemics? Ocean height, turbidity, and sea surface temperature can be observed and photographed from above and have often been linked to emerging epidemics. By examining photographs from past years as well as the data giving the numbers of cholera cases during those years, it has been shown that there is an increase in the numbers of cholera cases when the sea surface temperature is elevated and the ocean height is high.

NASA scientists relate that this information connects changes in climate such as the El Niño effect to cholera outbreaks. They are continuing to gather information about increased growth of algae in seas and possible relationships to cholera epidemics.

Source: http://geo.arc.nasa.gov/sge

One of the first breakthroughs using this satellite-based technology was the discovery that data on sea surface temperatures could be used to predict outbreaks of cholera in coastal areas. It was found that the cholera bacteria can survive in the hindquarters of common saltwater crustaceans called copepods. Remote-sensing systems detected zooplankton blooms (containing the copepods) and this was correlated with cholera risk in nearby coastal areas. More recently, cholera dissemination in Africa has been correlated with wind direction. It supports the idea that aeroplankton can bring cholera bacteria from one body of water to another. Aeroplankton are tiny life forms that can be carried by air currents.[6]

The heart of this new technology begins with mapping, just as Snow did so many years ago. His insight and inspiration started with the study of cholera in London and used methods still in use today. This has led to the study of global disease transmission using satellite and computer technologies today.

4

Transmission and Epidemiology of Cholera

A 27-year-old male suddenly developed severe diarrhea in November, 2003, in Lusaha, Zambia. He was visiting friends there and had been careful not to drink local water, as he had heard rumors of cholera outbreaks in the area. He went to one of the newly opened cholera treatment centers where he was diagnosed and treated for cholera. He got treatment and was able to go home in a few days.

While there he learned that health care workers were gathering evidence to track down this cholera outbreak. They had found that stool cultures were positive for Vibrio cholera O1 *in 74 percent of patients treated. That statistic included him. He was interviewed by authorities trying to locate the source of the outbreak. He was asked if he had eaten a local delicacy, kapenta—a sardine-like food staple. He had tried this delicacy on his visit, and he also indicated that he had eaten fresh, raw vegetables. The scientists told him that they had asked these same questions to hundreds of patients at this clinic and that they found that those who had eaten raw vegetables were more likely to get cholera than those who consumed kapenta or even some untreated water. In this instance, raw vegetables were the source of the epidemic.*

THE TRANSMISSION OF CHOLERA

Cholera epidemics have been associated with seasonal changes near estuaries. *Vibrio cholerae* is found in aquatic, particularly in estuary, areas around the world. Large numbers of *V. cholerae* are found in human populations during epidemics, but these bacteria are not found in

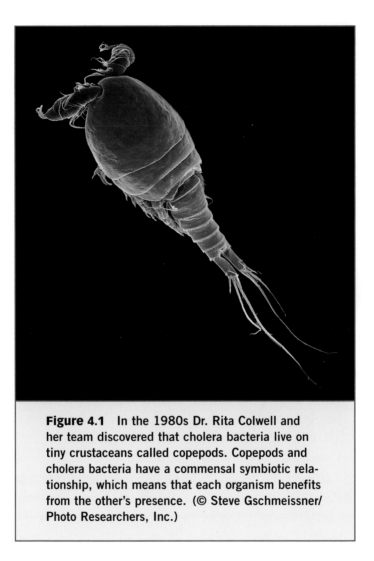

Figure 4.1 In the 1980s Dr. Rita Colwell and her team discovered that cholera bacteria live on tiny crustaceans called copepods. Copepods and cholera bacteria have a commensal symbiotic relationship, which means that each organism benefits from the other's presence. (© Steve Gschmeissner/ Photo Researchers, Inc.)

water environments near the outbreaks. This mystery was solved in the 1980s by the discovery that *V. cholerae* survives in dormant, unculturable forms in oceans between epidemics. In this dormant form the organism will not grown in lab cultures and thus can be difficult to identify. Further, Dr. Rita Colwell and her colleagues at the University of Maryland discovered that *V. cholerae* lives inside and on the bodies of common copepods, both in the Bay of Bengal and in the Chesapeake Bay. Copepods, which are relatives of shrimp, are part of the zooplankton, the microscopic plant and animal life in oceans. It has been estimated that a single copepod can carry 10,000 to as many as 100,000 *V. cholerae* bacteria.[1, 2]

How do *V. cholerae* bacteria live on copepods? Clusters of cholera bacteria have been found around the mouth and egg casings of female copepods. There the bacteria secretes a substance that helps the copepod's egg casing to rupture. This kind of symbiotic interaction is **commensal**, with each participant benefiting from the relationship.[3, 4]

Typically, epidemics occur in the spring or fall, when sea surface temperatures rise and rains and floods carry nutrients from rivers into estuaries and down toward the sea. This results in an increase in zooplankton populations. These conditions occurred during the El Niño in 1991 and 1992.

Using remote sensing to track zooplankton blooms, Colwell later predicted that there would not be a cholera outbreak after the tsunami in Southeast Asia in 2004. The tsunami occurred in December when the ocean temperature was low and did not support heavy growth of plankton populations and, hence, did not provide a host for *V. cholerae*.

Although the temperate phage CTX can infect a strain of cholera bacteria and provide it with genes for it to make cholera toxin, there are many virulent phage strains found in the environment of the bacteria as well. It is thought that these second interactions, the parasitism of lytic phages on bacterial cells, are going on during outbreaks as well. It is likely that as the bacterial populations increase during an epidemic, the populations of virulent phages increase also. Gradually these lytic phages take over, the bacteria are killed, and an epidemic subsides. This may explain the short duration of most cholera outbreaks.

Another set of observations describes **quorum sensing** in *V. cholerae*. Quorum sensing is the ability of bacteria to regulate gene expression as the cell density of a bacterial population changes. Chemical signals are sent out by bacteria to neighboring cells in a population. As the cell population increases, these signals shut down the production of virulence factors cholera toxin and TCP. These signals also act to control the formation of biofilms of bacteria during infections. Biofilms, or mats, of these bacteria are more likely to survive passing through the acidic human stomach, thus better surviving in the host. Quorum sensing within biofilms causes the release of single cells from the mats. These single cells form virulence factors in the host. As they grow to higher densities, quorum-sensing signals then shut off production of toxin and other virulence factors, and bacteria are then excreted to find another host.[5, 6]

PERSON TO PERSON

Unaware of these mechanisms of cholera transmission, Dr. Snow was still able to describe the connection between water supply and cholera infections. He did this through careful observation of the location of disease sufferers and by adhering to the scientific method. This was the groundwork for many studies of epidemics and the spread of diseases. It is remarkable that Snow's insights came before scientists knew, or even accepted the fact, that cholera is caused by a microorganism.

It is known that cholera infection is a result of transmission from environmental contamination to an individual, or from one individual to another. Poor sanitation methods lead to the contamination of soil, food, or water with *Vibrio cholerae* bacilli from feces. The cycle of transmission is complete when a person becomes a carrier. Individuals who are recovering from the disease may feel better but they still carry the microorganism within their bodies. These people are known as convalescent carriers. People who harbor the microorganism but do not yet show signs and symptoms of the disease are called incubatory carriers. They are also important in the transmission cycle of cholera.

Experiments using volunteers have shown that a dose of 10^3 (1,000) *Vibrio cholerae* cells are required to infect a person. These bacteria may come from contaminated water or from contaminated food, such as vegetables grown in human waste fertilizer. Cholera may also be spread directly from person to person. This often occurs when a cholera patient is being treated at home or when a cholera victim is being prepared for burial. *Vibrio cholerae* can survive on the body or clothing of a victim; thus the bacilli may be passed to anyone in close contact with the body. Because the disease causes profuse, watery diarrhea, cholera patients excrete many liters of fluid each day, and this fluid contains about 10^6 to 10^8 (1,000,000 to 100,000,000) cholera bacteria per milliliter. Therefore, contact with cholera patients poses a considerable risk of infection.

Cholera bacteria can be killed by heat, but they survive in the cold. They can live for two or more weeks in food such as milk, cooked rice, and seafood. They are sensitive to acidity but survive in alkaline environments. Thus, there are many opportunities for infection through food and drink.

THE HISTORY OF CHOLERA

Scholars do not entirely agree on the origin of the word *cholera*. It has been suggested that the word *cholera* is derived from the Greek words for bile (*cholera*) and flow (*rein*). Others suggest that in Greek the word *cholera* (which can also be interpreted as "roof gutter") probably indicates symptoms of water flow like that after a heavy rain. Cholera has been documented several times throughout history. A disease with symptoms similar to those of cholera is described in Sanskrit documents dating from about 500 B.C. to 400 B.C. Cholera was described early in the sixteenth century by European arrivals to India. It was documented by a staff member of the explorer Vasco da Gama that 20,000 men died of cholera in the early 1500s.

Since 1817, researchers have documented cholera epidemics all across the world. A worldwide epidemic is called a **pandemic**.

Other patterns of disease spread have also been observed for cholera. If the disease is present at a low, persistent level in a population, it is said to be **endemic**. The first cholera pandemic occurred as a result of wars between Persia and Turkey when soldiers were traveling between their native lands and would unknowingly carry the disease with them. The second pandemic is thought to have originated in Russia and spread to the Americas, reaching New York on June 23, 1832. The disease traveled to Philadelphia, and eventually to New Orleans. It was during this second pandemic, when it passed through London, that Dr. Snow made his observations that would ultimately connect water to cholera transmission.

Cholera first appeared in Chicago, Illinois, in 1849 when it was brought to the city via a boat carrying immigrants. From this point on, cholera epidemics occurred regularly in the city. City officials attempted to improve sanitation by using water from nearby Lake Michigan rather than local wells, which were often contaminated by sewage from the Chicago River. In 1867 the city opened a two-mile-long tunnel that carried water from the lake into the city. This further reduced the amount of sewage from the river into the local water supply.

NEW YORK: THE 1892 CHOLERA PANIC

By the 1890s, public awareness of cholera had grown significantly. In August 1892, emigrants from Hamburg, Germany, arrived in New York City. At that time, cholera was raging in Europe. Upon arrival, these ships were quarantined and steerage passengers were sent to special quarantine hospitals. Cabin passengers traveling first and second class were not allowed off the ship for 20 days. The passengers were not happy with this decision. They wanted to disembark right away because some of the workers on the ship were ill with cholera, and the passengers feared infection. The governor of New York decided to buy an unused hotel and the surrounding 120 acres of land in Babylon and Islip Town on Long Island for the quarantined passengers.

The local residents felt threatened because they were afraid that they would catch the disease, too. They took up weapons and threatened arson and other forms of violence if the governor allowed the boat passengers to stay in their towns. When the ship tried to dock, an angry mob of about 400 people stood waiting. They had sailed across the bay to the island where the hotel was located to confront the authorities. A state Supreme Court judge issued an injunction against the landing, and the mob went back home, satisfied. The National Guard and Naval Reserve were called in to keep peace. Eventually, a few of the quarantined passengers were allowed to disembark without incident.

This incident shows how the fear of infection can cause hysteria. Remember that this was during a time when little was known about this disease except that it made people very sick and could kill. The town residents were afraid because they did not know how they could protect themselves from cholera, and at that time, a cure did not exist.

Incidentally, the property that was purchased by the governor of New York remained in the hands of the state. The state legislature turned it into a park in 1908. It was the first state park on Long Island, and it still exists today as part of Robert Moses State Park.

TWENTIETH-CENTURY EPIDEMICS

By the 1900s, many people thought that improved sanitation would have prevented the recurrence of cholera. However, outbreaks continued sporadically and pandemics continued to occur, particularly in areas of poor sanitation. A 1961 pandemic was the result of a new **biovar**, or biotype variety of the bacterium, called the El Tor type. This biovar does not cause as severe an infection as the classic *Vibrio cholerae* O1, and it is still present to this day on six continents.

In 1992 a new serogroup of cholera appeared. Labeled Serogroup O139, it is nearly identical to the El Tor biovar but has several distinct characteristics. The emergence of this strain (also called the Bengal strain) in Madras (now Chennai), India, was a shift in the strains causing epidemics globally. Previously epidemics were caused primarily by the O1 serotype strain. Research indicated that this strain acquired new genetic segments horizontally. Scientists discovered that in the new O139 strain, 22 kilobases of DNA are missing from chromosome 1, and a new 35 kilobases segment of DNA has been added. While both strains O1 and O139 produced cholera toxin, the lipopolysaccharide (LPS) of the strains differed. Further, strain O139 (Bengal strain) has a polysaccharide capsule. Using DNA technologies, it was shown that the DNA fragment introduced into strain O139 carried genes for capsule synthesis. The Bengal strain was formed by horizontal transmission of DNA to the El Tor biotype of strain O1.

Genes for TCP (toxin coregulated pilus) are located on a region of genes called a large **pathogenicity island**. This is a DNA fragment greater than 30 kilobases in size that carries genes for virulent traits. This DNA is related to a phage, VPI (vibrio pathogenicity island), and it has been suggested that this DNA fragment has directed synthesis of TCP, which provides a coat protein for adhesion as well as a receptor site for CTX phage. This is an example of mechanisms that this bacterium has to evolve new strains through horizontal transmission.

Strain O139 is virulent because its capsule can make the microbe resist phagocytosis by host cells. Since the LPS is not like that of strain O1, many persons in populations had no immunity to it. In addition, this strain was found to have a plasmid that gives it resistance to many antibiotics.

THE STUDY OF EPIDEMICS AND PANDEMICS

Before researchers can study epidemics and pandemics, they must agree on how to define death from cholera (as opposed to death from other causes). The Pan American Health Organization defines this as "death within one week of onset of diarrhea in a person with confirmed or clinically defined cholera."[7]

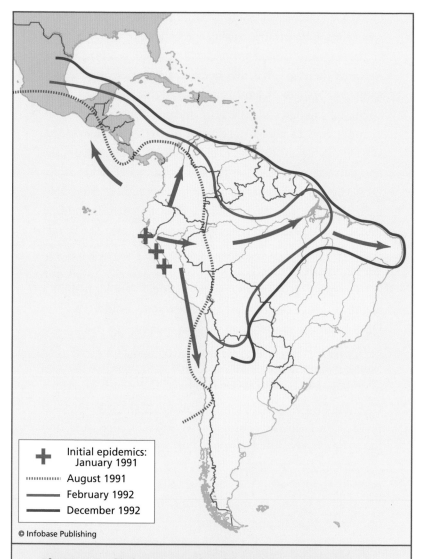

Figure 4.2 Cholera spread throughout Central and South America in 1991. This map shows the route of disease transmission. The epidemic was thought to be the result of ballast water exchange from ships in the area, but this was never proved.

While not every agency agrees with this definition, there has been an international effort to describe **mortality** data, i.e., the number of people who died from a specific disease. The World Health Organization (WHO) collects surveillance data about diseases from many countries. Cholera was the first disease for which this kind of international surveillance was organized.

The number of cases reported is less than the actual number of cases that occur. This is due to the fact that the definition of "case"—a person who actually has the disease—varies considerably. Because there are many causes for diarrhea, the issue is even more unclear. The **morbidity** rate, or the number of cases of infection, should be confined to those cases for which there has been a positive laboratory diagnosis, but this does not always happen. Some countries cannot afford to test everyone who should be tested. Researchers believe that there are 10 times more actual cases of cholera worldwide than the number of cases reported. Therefore, morbidity rate data are suspect without standardized definitions.

The **incidence** of infections, or new cases, with cholera is dependent on the condition of the area, the opportunities for transmitting the bacterium, and the numbers of those immune in the population. Most people who harbor cholera bacilli within their body do not show symptoms and are thus labeled as **asymptomatic**. One estimate is that just 2 percent of new cases are severe, 5 percent are moderate, and 18 percent have mild symptoms. Up to 75 percent of cases are asymptomatic.[8,9]

Since such a large number of bacteria are necessary for infection, cholera is usually not transmitted without food or water contamination. Researchers have observed that caregivers usually do not become infected. This shows that sanitary precautions are important in the control of the disease. Often it is possible to trace the source of an epidemic, but not always. In one example, the Latin American epidemic of

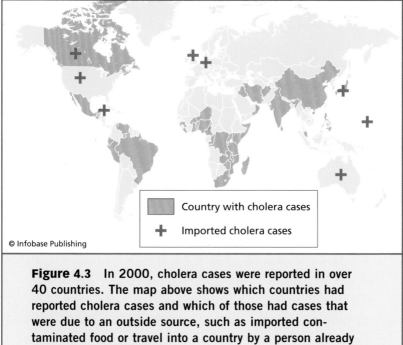

© Infobase Publishing

Figure 4.3 In 2000, cholera cases were reported in over 40 countries. The map above shows which countries had reported cholera cases and which of those had cases that were due to an outside source, such as imported contaminated food or travel into a country by a person already infected with the disease.

1991 is thought to have come from ballast water, but scientists could not prove this theory.

Scientists study the geographic distribution of disease infections because this will help them to better understand the disease itself. In 1993, the incidence of cholera was highest in Central and South America, Africa, and the sub-Asian continent (India, Pakistan, Bangladesh, and China). Cholera is a seasonal disease; its occurrence is rare in cooler months. The peak incidence in India is before the monsoon season in Kolkata and after the monsoon season in Chennai (farther south). In Bangladesh, the peak season for El Tor cholera is in the fall, while the peak for the classical biotype is from December to January. Age and sex of a person have no effect on whether or not they will become infected if they do not have immunity to the disease. It has been observed that individuals with type O blood are more likely to become infected and will have a more severe case of the disease than people with other blood types. The reason for this is unknown.

Other settings where cholera occurs include religious migrations and at refugee camps due to the close proximity of all the inhabitants. Cholera is also associated with extreme poverty. Since cholera bacilli are sensitive to gastric acid, any impairment of the formation of gastric acid will increase the possibility of cholera infection. This can include stomach surgery or use of antacids or anti-ulcer medications.

CHOLERA IN THE UNITED STATES TODAY

Although rare, cases of cholera do occasionally occur in the United States. In 1991, three cases of cholera were found in Maryland. They were associated with the consumption of frozen coconut milk imported from Asia. The affected individuals had not traveled outside the United States. They had not eaten raw shellfish in the preceding month. However, all of the affected individuals had attended the same private party where they ate crabs and rice pudding with coconut milk. Unopened packages of the same brand of coconut milk (but a different shipment), which had been imported from Asia, were examined. Cholera bacteria were found within the food.

In this same year, 16 other cases occurred in the United States. All of the individuals affected had recently traveled to ether South America or to Asia. Of these, two were infected with the same biotype as those infected in Maryland from the coconut milk imported from Asia. Other outbreaks included isolation of *Vibrio cholerae* O1 from oysters in Mobile Bay, Alabama, in 1991–1992.

International travel has led to an increased number of cholera cases in the United States. In 1992, about one case of cholera was being reported each week. Here is an example of such a case, as was discovered by the Connecticut Department of Health. A 43-year-old woman traveled with her two teenage daughters to Ecuador over the Christmas holidays. The mother ate raw clams and one of the daughters ate shrimp. The next evening, the mother ate cooked crab and lobster, and the same teenage daughter ate cooked crab. The other daughter ate no seafood at all during the trip. The mother had onset of vomiting, cramps, and diarrhea 16 hours after the second meal. The older teenage daughter developed similar symptoms 12 hours later. The younger daughter did not get sick. Both the mother and the older daughter were treated with intravenous fluids and antimicrobial medication. Toxic El Tor *Vibrio* bacteria were isolated from both individuals.

Although cholera is rare in the United States, it is still possible to contract the disease. The most common methods of transmission, especially for people residing in developed countries with good sanitation methods, is by eating contaminated seafood and/or traveling to regions where cholera is common. However, despite the few recent outbreaks, cholera is not an immediate public health problem in the United States as it is in many undeveloped countries.

RECENT CHOLERA

The World Health Organization (WHO) reported that the number of cholera cases rose dramatically in 2006. There were a total of 236,896 cases reported from 52 countries. This number included 6,311 deaths. This level of cases had not been reported since the late 1990s.

This number of cases is an increase of 79 percent over the under-reported numbers of 2005. Cholera is under-reported for a wide variety of reasons: lack of funding, desire to protect a nation's image, or geographical remoteness. Attempts to document cases indicate that less than 10 percent of cases are reported to WHO. There were 130,000 deaths from cholera reported in 1998; 20,000 in 2001; and 70,000 in 2005. The dramatic increase in deaths from cholera in 2006 indicates that the disease remains a global threat.[10]

Signs and Symptoms of Cholera

John had rushed to make his flight to London from the Lima, Peru, airport. He started feeling ill during the long flight. He visited the London airport's doctor and told her of his symptoms: he had been experiencing diarrhea for the past 18 to 24 hours, was very tired, nauseous, dehydrated, and had no fever; his blood pressure dropped a bit when he stood. The airport doctor asked John what he had been doing in Peru. John said that he was doing fieldwork in a refuge camp located in the foothills of the Andes Mountains. He said that the conditions there were primitive and that clean water was scarce. The doctor started John on oral liquid therapy at once, and she sent John to a local clinic where he took tests and a diagnosis of cholera was confirmed. John was prescribed a tetracycline antibiotic, to help him recover faster.

THE GENERAL PATTERN OF CLASSIC CHOLERA

After cholera bacilli infect and establish themselves in an individual, there is a period of time from one to three days, called the **incubation period**, before symptoms appear. The first symptoms of classic *Vibrio cholerae* infection are the rapid but painless onset of watery diarrhea and vomiting. Loss of fluids through the stool can be copious. As much as one liter of fluid can be lost per hour, even though it is often much less. Along with water, the patient will also lose essential salts such as sodium and potassium (Figure 5.1).

Diarrhea is caused by adherence of *Vibrio cholerae* bacteria to the **epithelium** of the upper small bowel. The microbes do not appear to

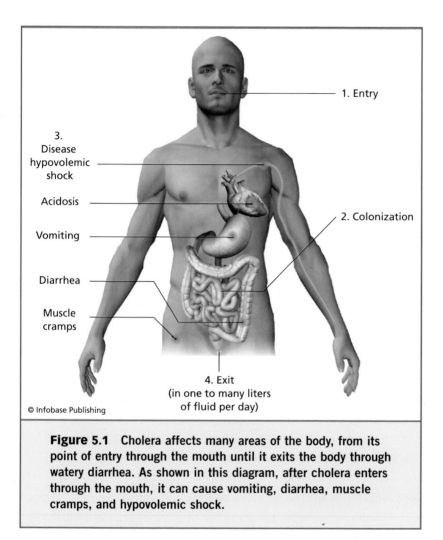

1. Entry

3.
Disease
hypovolemic
shock

Acidosis

Vomiting

Diarrhea

Muscle
cramps

2. Colonization

4. Exit
(in one to many liters
of fluid per day)

© Infobase Publishing

Figure 5.1   Cholera affects many areas of the body, from its point of entry through the mouth until it exits the body through watery diarrhea. As shown in this diagram, after cholera enters through the mouth, it can cause vomiting, diarrhea, muscle cramps, and hypovolemic shock.

invade the intestinal cells and tissues, and there is no visible damage to the mucosal cells of the intestine. In addition, bacilli do not usually enter the bloodstream, which would induce a condition known as **bacteremia**. The watery stools often contain white flecks of sloughed off tissue and white blood cells, and are referred to as "rice water stools" because of this appearance. This loss of fluid leads to an intense thirst, which begins once the amount of lost fluid equals 2 to 3 percent of the patient's body weight. Severe dehydration can be prevented with rehydration therapy.

The first sign of dehydration is the loss of skin elasticity. This is due to the loss of fluid from the subcutaneous tissues (tissue right underneath the skin). The skin will lose its elasticity when 5 to 10 percent of the patient's body weight has been lost in fluid. If one picks up a fold of skin, it does not fall quickly back into place. This is loss of **skin turgor**. This is most easily seen in healthy individuals who show loose skin over the abdomen. Wrinkling of the skin on the fingers is also commonly observed. Eyes often appear sunken as a result of loss of skin turgor, too. However, sunken eyes as a result of a loss of skin turgor may not be a sign of dehydration in starving children or in the elderly because that is also a sign of starvation.

When the amount of lost fluid reaches more than 10 percent of the body weight, blood volume levels drop, specifically in the serum. This is called **hypovolemia**. There is a serious loss of fluid in the extracellular compartments of the body and also in the volume of circulating blood. Dehydration also causes a loss of **electrolytes**, such as sodium, potassium, bicarbonate, and chloride. Blood pressure drops and the pulse rate may be greater than 100 beats per minute. The arm pulse is low, sometimes not even detectable. Pulses at the femoral artery in the leg region and the carotid artery in the neck region are usually still present, however. The arms and the legs become cold. The rectal temperature is often elevated. The fingers become shriveled and wrinkled, a phenomenon called washer women's hands. The tips of the tongue and lips may be blue, the mouth is dry, and the eyes are sunken into their sockets. The voice is hoarse. Patients complain about pains and cramps in the arms and legs, and sometimes even in the muscles of the abdomen.

Bowel sounds occur and they may vary from infrequent and somewhat mild to frequent and active. The abdomen is

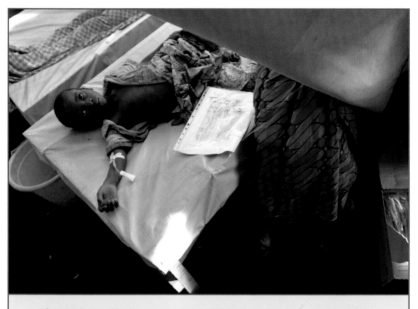

Figure 5.2   Cholera spreads quickly in refugee camps, where sanitation is often lacking. The boy shown here contracted cholera in a Congolese refugee camp and is being treated at a medical center run by Doctors Without Borders (Médecins Sans Frontieres). (© Lionel Healing/AFP/Getty Images)

not usually tender. Patients with severe cholera usually remain conscious but occasionally coma occurs.

The loss of electrolytes through watery stools leads to other signs of cholera, if untreated. There is concentration of blood in the serum. **Oliguria**, which refers to urinating less than usual, occurs. **Acidosis**, a lowering of the pH of blood plasma, occurs as well. Acidosis is responsible for the labored and erratic breathing. Another result of hypovolemia is possible kidney, or renal, failure.

Hypoglycemia, the lowering of the blood glucose levels, occurs as a complication of many diarrheal diseases, including cholera. Half of children with cholera develop hypoglycemia. Forty percent of children who reach this stage of the disease will die. The reason for this complication in some but not all severe cholera patients is not known. It may reflect a difference in nutrition, fasting, or enzyme failures. Loss of potassium can cause paralysis and erratic heartbeat. Seizures of unknown origin sometimes occur in children, also. The third-trimester fetus of pregnant mothers with cholera will die about 50 percent of the time. Most deaths from cholera occur within the first 24 hours of infections. However, nearly all of these horrid signs and symptoms can be avoided with proper and timely treatment.

VARIOUS MANIFESTATIONS OF CHOLERA

Cases of cholera may vary in severity. Some cases are mild, and the body is able to recover in three to four days. In this case, the disease is called a **self-limiting infection**. More severe cases can result in death in 50 percent of the cases if the patients are not treated. Death is mainly the result of severe dehydration. If the patient receives proper treatment, the fatality rate is less than one percent. Most patients who recover from the disease get rid of the bacteria in their bodies in two weeks or less. However, some do not, and these people become convalescent carriers. They harbor microbes in bile ducts and shed them into their fecal material. In this way, they can supply cholera bacilli to others in the population, even though they themselves no longer have symptoms of the disease.

THE HOST-PARASITE RELATIONSHIP

The relationship between a host and a parasite is a complex and delicate balancing act. A good analogy is that the host and parasite are children on a seesaw, with the host on one side and the microbe, or parasite, on the other. The balance can be tipped to favor either the host or the microbe. If the microbe is particularly strong, or virulent, or exists in particularly high numbers, it may get the upper hand, lowering the patient's resistance, thus increasing the chances of illness. If the patient has lost his or her ability to combat infections, the microbe is strongly favored. On the other hand, if the immune system is strong and healthy or if the patient receives treatment, the balance may be restored, the patient gets the upper hand, and the illness wanes.

Obviously this relationship is not that simple, since so many factors come into play. For instance, microbes may possess the ability to form toxins, they may have a very rapid growth rate, they may be invasive, they may avoid the **phagocytic cells** of the immune defense system, or they may be able to adhere to a specific site in the patient's tissue. Sometimes the genetic makeup of the microorganism changes and it becomes more virulent. In contrast, human factors that play a role in this relationship and may be characteristics of the host include general health, age, the quality of nutrition, the **normal flora** (bacteria that normally reside in the host), a strong immune system, and the treatments the host might receive.

CASE STUDIES

In 2001, case reports from three patients with cholera were presented in the Centers for Disease Control and Prevention's (CDC) online journal, *Emerging Infectious Diseases*.[1] It appeared that a new type of cholera had emerged. The case involved twin boys. Both boys died despite being treated with antibiotics (penicillin and gentamicin). The first boy died within three days of his birth, and *Vibrio cholera* O1 was isolated from his blood. The second boy followed the same course of the illness and died two days after his brother. The second child's blood sample was negative. The mother did not have any diarrhea and doctors were unable to collect a stool sample.

In another case, a 65-year-old woman fell ill with profuse watery diarrhea and visited a rural health center. She was fed intravenously but was not given antibiotics. Her diarrhea stopped and she was sent home. However over the next three days, she developed anuria (inability to urinate), confusion, and chills. When she was admitted to a larger hospital, she had no fever, but she was dehydrated, confused, and in shock. She was given intravenous rehydration and antibiotics (chloramphenicol and gentamicin). Blood tests revealed elevated white blood cells, lowered sodium and potassium, and elevated urea. *Vibrio cholerae* was grown from her blood sample. This strain was sensitive to erythromycin but resistant to many other antibiotics. The antibiotic therapy was changed. After treatment with erythromycin the blood cultures, rectal swab, and urine culture were negative. She was rehydrated and had good urine output but remained in renal failure. She died 14 days after being admitted to the hospital.

In another case, a 45-year-old woman with profuse, watery diarrhea was admitted to the hospital. She was dehydrated and had no fever, but she had an erratic heartbeat. She was given oral rehydration therapy. When her diarrhea became bloody, doctors took a culture and began antibiotic therapy. The diarrhea stopped over the next 36 hours and she could move about, but on day four she suddenly collapsed and died. After her death, *Vibrio cholerae* O1 was isolated from her blood. A stool sample was not collected.

In 1998, the first case of cholera imported to Japan was found. A 20-year-old female was referred from Osaka airport to the general Hospital of Osaka City. She had traveled in Thailand and Indonesia the previous week. On March 11, she had developed watery diarrhea. The diarrhea occurred four to six times a day until her admission to the hospital two days later. The patient did not have nausea, vomiting, or fever. Her serum potassium was low, probably a result of the diarrhea. A stool sample taken on admission to the hospital indicated the presence of both *V. cholerae* O1 and O139 strains. The different strains were detected by slide agglutination tests. It can also be shown that strains are different by comparing the specific base sequences in the bacterial DNA and examining for the presence of the specific base sequence that is known for the determination of the amino acid sequence in the cholera toxin.

After three days of treatment, which included the administration of the antibiotic ofloxacin, the two cholera strains were no longer isolated and the patient's diarrhea disappeared. Sensitivities of the two strains to different antibiotics were tested and found to be dissimilar. Patterns of DNA sequences of the two strains were found to be very different. Therefore, it was concluded that the patient was infected with both strains of cholera bacteria.[2]

In this case, some newer methods of diagnosis were performed. Since the amino acid sequence for the protein of cholera toxin (CT) is known, the DNA sequence for it can be deduced from the genetic code. This sequence of nucleotides can be chemically synthesized in the laboratory. Now, the total DNA from a strain isolated from a patient can be tested to see if the DNA probe can bind to a sequence from that bacterial DNA. If this occurs, then the bacteria isolated contain the gene for cholera toxin.

THE DIAGNOSIS OF CHOLERA

Vibrio cholerae is easily isolated and identified in a bacteriology laboratory. A patient with severe diarrhea and exhibiting symptoms of cholera can be diagnosed in a few minutes by examining a stool sample and finding rapidly motile bacteria using a microscope. A preparation of bacteria can be prepared and a drop of antiserum containing anti-*V. cholerae* O group 1 antibodies. This will stop movement of the bacteria after binding to them when they contain the antigen receptor for these antibodies.

A variation of this technique is the use of antiserum to which a fluorescent chemical (fluorescein) has been chemically bound. This fluorescent antibody can be added directly to a stool or rectal swab smear on a slide. If bacteria containing these antigens are present, the bacteria will fluoresce, or glow, when examined with a microscope under ultraviolet light.

Most *Vibrios* form a mucus-like string when a colony is mixed in 0.5 percent sodium deoxycholate solution. This is called a string test, and it can be used when cholera bacteria are suspected but do not agglutinate with antisera preparations.

Strains also can be isolated from cholera patients by growth on TCBS agar (thiosulfate-citrate-bile salts-sucrose). To isolate cholera bacteria from the environment (soil and water) or from carriers (persons infected with cholera bacteria who have no symptoms), it is recommended that samples be placed in alkaline (pH 8.5) peptone broth and incubated for six hours. This will provide conditions for rapid growth of *Vibrio* species while suppressing growth of other bacteria in a sample. The growth in the peptone broth is then streaked onto appropriate agar plates. The technique is called an enrichment procedure.

WHY DIAGNOSE AFTER TREATMENT?

A patient will be treated and, it is hoped, cured of cholera before a definitive diagnosis can be made. However, making

CHOLERA AND HISTORY

We will probably never know the effects of cholera throughout history. We can speculate that the impact of cholera and cholera-like infections must have been considerable in historical times. Historians have estimated that crusaders of the eleventh to thirteenth centuries were defeated by bacteria more than by the Saracens. Napoleon's soldiers retreating from Russia were decimated by infectious diseases that gave them diarrhea.

Researchers have documented that President James K. Polk died of cholera in 1849. Another death from cholera is more controversial. The Russian composer Peter Ilych Tchaikovsky (*Swan Lake*, *Sleeping Beauty*, *The Nutcracker*) died of cholera. A troubled man, some have suggested that he drank contaminated water intentionally, thus committing suicide.

the diagnosis is valuable because it is vital to track epidemics of the disease, follow control methods, and identify any new strains that may appear. Because treatment and diagnosis occur simultaneously, it is difficult to obtain good information about case numbers of cholera, since cholera often ends up being underreported. Cholera symptoms are similar to those of other infections of the gastrointestinal tract. After a patient is cured and sent home, there may not be a follow-up to identify specific strains. Countries dependent on tourism dollars may be reluctant to publish information about cholera cases. For these reasons, rapid diagnostic tests can be important to help trace outbreaks of the disease.

Dipstick tests for rapid diagnosis of cholera have been described. The antibodies on dipstick rectal swabs can detect trace amounts of cholera. The dipsticks can be stored at room temperature in plastic bags. They are easy to use, and tests can be read in about 10 minutes. Tests are highly specific and very sensitive to detect cholera.[3]

Since cholera is often found in areas or situations where laboratory facilities are not available, this type of test will be valuable to improve reporting cases of cholera. This, in turn, will help monitor the appearance and spread of cholera epidemics.

These examples show that, while symptoms of cholera make diagnosis easy, not all patients are the same. Some show bacteria present in the blood, called bacteremia, while others do not. One patient did not suffer from diarrhea, one suffered from only short-lived bloody diarrhea, and another suffered renal failure after treatment. We may never know what causes these differences. However, tools for identification of strains of bacteria help to trace the appearance of new variants of bacteria, so that medical science can provide treatments as fast as bacteria can find new ways to overcome hosts and to upset the delicate balance of the host-parasite relationship.

6

The Virulence of
Vibrio cholerae

The **virulence** of a microorganism describes its ability to cause severe disease. A disease, or the state of having a disease, is a condition whereby the physiology of the body is distinct from a normal, healthy state. **Pathogenic** refers to a microorganism's ability to cause such disease symptoms. A microbe can be pathogenic but not virulent if it causes a mild form of a disease. This would be a form of the disease with less harmful or uncomfortable symptoms. General features of pathogenic or virulent microorganisms are (1) the ability to attach to host cells, (2) the ability to escape host defenses, (3) the ability to obtain essential nutrients, and (4) the ability to produce symptoms.

WHAT ABOUT THE CHOLERA VIBRIO?

Vibrio cholerae bacteria adhere to the **villi** that line the small intestine (Figures 6.1a and 6.1b). The bacteria have special filaments that recognize carbohydrate receptors on the surface of the villi. The cholera bacillus produces a toxin (abbreviated CT, for cholera toxin) that binds to cell receptors (**gangliosides**) made of the **glycolipids**. These ganglioside receptors are called G_{M1} to identify them as a specific kind of ganglioside with a known chemical structure. One part of the toxin produced by the cholera bacillus is an enzyme. When the entire toxin binds to the receptors, the enzyme portion is removed and enters the host cell. Inside the cell, CT causes an increase in a chemical called **cyclic AMP** (cAMP).

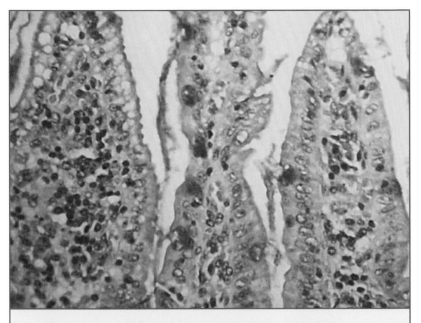

Figure 6.1a *Vibrio cholerae* attaches to the wall of the small intestine and causes increased mucous production. This electron micrograph shows a section of the intestinal wall. (Courtesy CDC)

THE WORKINGS OF CYCLIC AMP IN CHOLERA BACILLI

The chemical cAMP appears in small amounts in all cells in order to stimulate various proteins that respond to outside signals, such as hormones. It is formed from ATP, the common energy-carrying molecule in cells, and can be quickly removed by conversion to AMP after an enzyme attack. However, while the cAMP is present, it can stimulate proteins in cells. For example, it can stimulate cells to degrade more sugars and to form more ATP. A sudden stimulus, such as the need to move rapidly in response to a threat, can request cells to supply a source of chemical energy rapidly. This is often referred to as the fight-or-flight response in animals. AMP serves to stimulate the breakdown of glycogen and

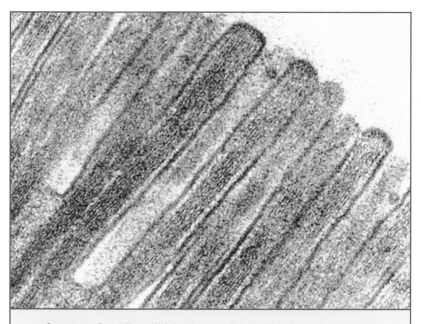

Figure 6.1b Microvilli in the small intestine increase surface area, which is ideal for nutrient absorption under normal circumstances. However, microvilli also provide an ideal place for the cholera bacilli to attach. (Courtesy Dartmouth College Rippel Electron Microscope Facility)

the formation of glucose, which is used as a source of quick energy. In gut cells, the response to cAMP is to change ion transport.

The body must activate the enzyme **adenyl cyclase** in order to form cAMP from ATP. The cAMP is then degraded by another enzyme, **phosphodiesterase**, to form AMP. AMP can be recycled in cells to form more ATP at another time as needed. If the cAMP remains high, the cell will be stimulated to excess. The reactions can be summarized in this way:

ATP ————————→ cAMP ————————→ AMP

        adenyl cyclase   phosphodiesterase

Adenyl cyclase is membrane-bound; it is activated by neighboring receptor sites that have received some signal in the form of a molecule binding to that receptor site. This changes the shape and activity of the bound adenyl cyclase so that it can form cAMP from the ATP that is usually found in most cells. Phosphodiesterase can be inhibited by chemicals that are similar to cAMP in structure. One such chemical is caffeine, a major compound in coffee. When too much caffeine is consumed, the phosphodiesterase can be blocked and cAMP accumulates. This can result it too much stimulation. That is what "coffee nerves" are all about!

Cyclic AMP inside intestinal cells overstimulates the sodium pumps located in the cell membranes of intestinal cells. There is first an outpouring of sodium ions (Na^+), and then of chloride ions (Cl^-). This creates an imbalance of ions across the cell membrane. In order to correct this imbalance, water flows across the membrane from the cells into the **lumen**, the intestinal tract space. This is the source of the diarrhea in cholera infections.

WHAT OTHER PROPERTIES HELP MAKE CHOLERA BACILLI VIRULENT?

In addition to toxin, cholera bacilli have **pili**, the short hairlike appendages on bacterial cells that are similar in structure to flagella. They help bacteria adhere to a surface, and they may be sites for the attachment of bacterial viruses in some cells. They are an important virulence factor for the cholera bacillus since they help attach the bacteria to intestinal cells.

The cholera bacillus has a sheathed flagellum at only one end, meaning it is single-polar. This can help the microbe to escape cells that would digest it, as well as to move toward sources of nutrients. The microbe produces proteins that can clump red blood cells, hemagglutinins, and mucinase, an enzyme that can break down **mucin**, a protective cell material. The mucinase helps the microorganism to break down the protective layer surrounding the intestinal cells, thus aiding its penetration. The role of hemagglutinins in virulence is less clear.

THE TOXIN

Of all the virulence factors, the formation of the adhering pili and the formation of the toxin are most essential for the pathogenicity of the cholera bacillus, i.e., its ability to make people ill. The toxin is essential for the major symptoms of cholera. This toxin is **oligomeric**, meaning that it is composed of several proteins. It is secreted across the outer bacterial membrane of the Gram negative cholera bacilli into the external environment that surrounds the bacterial cells. Two proteins form a structure called the A subunit. Five other proteins form a portion of the toxin called the B subunit. Each protein in the B subunit is identical and forms a pentagonal (five-sided) structure with a hole in the center and is therefore referred to as a donut. There are two parts to the A protein, subunit A_1 and subunit A_2. These are connected by a disulfide bond. Subunit A_2 is a long protein docked within the donut of the B portion of the proteins. It has a structure called an α-*helix* (**alpha-helix**). This structure is a coiled configuration of the protein chains; each third amino acid in the sequence is held by hydrogen bonds to the first amino acid in a chain. It is often found in proteins as part of their structural architecture. This part of the A protein anchors it to the B proteins. The A_1 subunit is potentially an enzyme once it has been freed from the A_2 protein anchor.

The B protein pentamers bind to the receptor site of the intestinal cells. A_1 is then cut off from the rest of the protein and enters into the host (intestinal) cell. It is now an enzyme. The remaining toxin proteins now enter into the cell.

Cholera toxin is an AB toxin. AB toxins bind to plasma membrane receptors on host cells. These receptors can be proteins, glycoproteins, or glycolipids. Not all bacterial AB toxins enter cells in the same way. However, B fragments in AB toxins serve to deliver the A components of toxins by binding

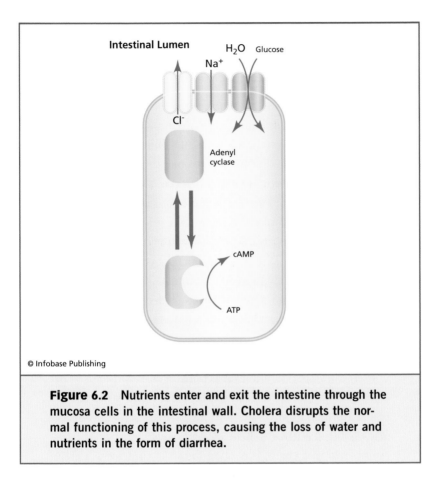

Intestinal Lumen H_2O Glucose

Na^+

Cl^-

Adenyl
cyclase

cAMP

ATP

Figure 6.2   Nutrients enter and exit the intestine through the mucosa cells in the intestinal wall. Cholera disrupts the normal functioning of this process, causing the loss of water and nutrients in the form of diarrhea.

to surface receptors and translocating the A fragment into the cytoplasm of the target cell.

Cholera toxin enters host cells by using a host membrane system designed to rid the cell of misfolded proteins. This system removes such defective proteins through a membrane system from the endoplasmic reticulum to the Golgi apparatus and finally outside of the cell. This system is partly reversible. The misfolded, defective proteins can be recycled by first binding to a complex to transport it back into the cell for recycling. A key protein of this complex is called sec61. Once the misfolded protein binds to sec61, it is transported back into the cell. There a substance, **ubiquitin**, is attached to the lysine amino acids in the defective protein, thus "labeling" the protein as defective. It is now recognized by degradation enzymes in the cytoplasm, and it is broken down to its amino acid components, which may be reused in cell metabolism.[1]

Cholera toxin A fragments resemble proteins that are misfolded. These fragments are transported through the existing complex, binding to protein sec61. Remarkably, there are few lysine amino acids in these fragments, so they are not labeled with ubiquitin and are not recognized by host degradation enzymes. Therefore, the toxin can enter the cytoplasm, ready to diffuse to the cell target ribosomes.

Some bacterial AB toxins use endocytosis pathways in host cells to enter cells. These include diphtheria, anthrax, and botulism toxins. Like cholera toxin, *Pseudomonas aeurginosa* exotoxin A and shiga toxin of some *Shigella* bacteria use the pathway from the endoplasmic reticulum for elimination of defective proteins by entering through pores in the cell membrane at the complex containing sec61 and other proteins.

THE STRUCTURE OF THE TOXIN

The chemistry and structure of the cholera toxin are well known. The protein has a mass of 85 kilodaltons and is comprised of 755 amino acids. The A subunit is 27,234 daltons in mass, while the B subunits are 11,677 daltons each. Five of these subunits comprise the total B subunit, 58,307 daltons in mass. The entire toxin, or **holotoxin**, is 85,620 daltons. The A subunit is made of 240 amino acids. It is cut by an enzyme that attacks peptide bonds in the center of amino acid sequences in proteins (**endopeptidase**) between amino acids number 193 and 195 to form the A_1 and A_2 subunits. The A_1 protein is wedge-shaped and is enzymatic. The B protein is more stable to changes in the environment than is the A protein, which is more loosely folded.

The B proteins bind to the carbohydrate chain on the ganglioside G_{M1} receptor. There are five carbohydrate sugars in this chain, and each one binds to a B protein. There is little change in the B protein after it is bound to the ganglioside.

Once the sequence of the amino acids in the toxin proteins was known, scientists could construct and visualize atomic models of these proteins in three dimensions. These pictures and diagrams show that once the cholera toxin A subunit (CTA1) enters the cell, it interacts with a protein known as adenosine diphosphate (ADP)-ribosylation factor 6 (ARF6). This protein is known to promote the activity of the toxin. When ARF6 is bound to GTP, the ARF6-GTP formed interacts with CTA1 and causes it to change shape, revealing the active site for the NAD+. Therefore, ARF6 is an allosteric activator of cholera toxin. It binds to a site other than the active site and causes changes in the activity of the toxin protein.[2]

THE FUNCTION OF THE TOXIN

A_1 is an enzyme. It is an ADP ribosyl transferase. The substrate of this enzyme is **NAD (nicotinamide adenine dinucleotide)**. This is a major electron carrier in cells, vital for energy metabolism. Therefore, it is produced in rather significant amounts in the cells. The A_1 enzyme splits the NAD into two portions of this molecule: nicotinamide and ADP-ribose. The ADP-ribose portion is then attached to a portion of the receptor protein on the intestinal cells, thereby altering its activity.

This receptor protein is called a G protein, because it uses **GTP** for its activity and control. The G protein is composed of three subunits called beta (β), alpha (α), and gamma (γ). After a hormone binds to a cell, this protein complex binds to GTP and then splits into a portion composed of beta and gamma, and another portion composed of alpha and GTP. These may recombine, lose a phosphate group, then release the GDP thus formed, and return to the hormone receptor site for reuse. The alpha protein with GTP stimulates the adenyl cyclase so that cAMP is formed.

When the cholera toxin is present, it attaches the ADP-ribose from NAD to the alpha-GTP protein, preventing it from recycling by release of a phosphate group. This inactivated alpha-GTP protein promotes dissociation of the G protein complex and inactivates an enzyme that can convert GTP to GDP (GTPase). The result is that cAMP formation continues, while the ability of the cell to turn off the formation of cAMP is lost. The G protein can no longer be recycled, and the formation of cAMP continues.

After toxin binding, it takes about 15 minutes before there is a rise in cAMP. This may be the time that the A protein is transported across the membrane and is split to form the free A_1 subunit. The alpha subunit of the G receptor protein binds to GTP, and this stimulates the sodium pump in gut cells. When it is inactivated by the cholera toxin, the alpha-GTP protein is stabilized while the GTPase activity decreases. The result is that the amount of cAMP increases. GTP and Mg^{++} are needed for the action of the toxin. GTP is needed on the complex, and the magnesium is required by enzymes that can synthesize GTP.

THE CHOLERA TOXIN AS A REAGENT

Since the mechanism and structure of the cholera toxin are well known, the toxin has been used as a reagent. A reagent is a substance used to test for the presence of other substances in a solution. In the case of cholera toxin, these uses exploit the ability of the B protein to bind to specific cells and to deliver a protein to those cells. If the A protein is removed and another protein substituted, then this B protein can be used as a reagent to deliver proteins other than the A_1 protein subunit to the interior of cells. It has been used to study ganglioside receptor sites, which are found in high concentration in membranes of neurons. Scientists have discovered that another protein, myelin basic protein, can be ribosylated by cholera toxin. This protein is a major part of myelin, which is found associated with nerve cells. Cholera toxin can be used to study myelin and myelin defects in nerve cells. Thus, a good understanding of this protein has made it useful for the study of other areas of the biological sciences.

Recent understanding of the way that cholera toxin enters cells using a transport channel system may improve future research in this area. Proteins that can unfold and yet lack lysine amino acids will emulate the uptake of cholera toxin. Proteins with these properties will be more likely to be imported into cells. There has been some success in the use of antibodies or portions of antibodies that target surface receptors to prepare immunotoxins that can kill some cancer cells. In some cases, AB toxins that enter by endocytosis have been used. The goals of this research are first to understand precisely how a bacterial toxin enters a cell, and then to modify the carrier protein required for entry such that a substance toxic to the target cell can be delivered, destroying that cell. Future research will undoubtedly use cholera and cholera-like toxins as well as other bacterial toxins as carriers to introduce toxic substances to specific host cells.

Once the cholera toxin binds to gut cells, it sets in motion a chain of events that disrupt normal cell functions. Cyclic AMP is a vital intermediate for hormones to instruct cells to perform specific tasks. The control of levels of cyclic AMP in intestinal cells by cholera toxin interferes with the levels of cyclic AMP formed, as well as the control of that formation.

7

The Genome of *Vibrio cholerae*

THE KNOWLEDGE PROVIDED BY AN ENTIRE GENOME

In the August 3, 2000, issue of the journal *Nature*, a research team at the Institute for Genomic Research (TIGR) in Maryland published the entire nucleic acid sequence of the genome of *Vibrio cholerae*. Determining the complete genetic code for any organisms is a major research breakthrough for understanding that organism. It offers the blueprint for all of the products that the organism can produce. Often, scientists will discover completely new genes in the process. In many cases, the functions of these genes are not yet known.

The nucleic acid sequence can be examined in a variety of ways. One way is to compare sequences with those from related organisms, which may allow possible amino acid sequences of unknown proteins to be determined. An important goal is to describe the **annotated sequence** for the genome, a description of the functions for the genes of an organism. In this way, scientists can discern information about likely structural features of the proteins that can be formed by the organism. For example, some nucleic acid sequence patterns strongly indicate that a region of a protein may be folded into an α-helix structure. The nucleic acid sequence data can be examined for potential evolutionary origins of genes.

THE UNIQUENESS OF THE GENOME OF *VIBRIO CHOLERAE*

The genome of the cholera bacillus is comprised of two circular chromosomes. This is unusual, since most bacteria have a single circular chromosome. Chromosome 1 has 2,961,146 nucleic acid base pairs, and Chromosome 2 has 1,072,914 base pairs. These base pairs comprise a total of 3,885 **open reading frames** (**ORFs**). An open reading frame is a coding sequence between an **initiator** and a **terminator codon**. It is necessary to find the sequence of bases that is the site for ribosome binding and that precedes the initiator codon. Open reading frames allow scientists to locate numbers of gene groups in an organism.

HOW ARE GENES DISTRIBUTED
BETWEEN THE TWO CHROMOSOMES?

On Chromosome 1, 58 percent of the 962 ORFs code for proteins that are known, and 6 percent code for proteins that are known but for which there are no known functions. Seventeen percent of the ORFs contain sequences similar to other known ORFs, but scientists do not yet know if the cholera bacillus actually makes these gene products. Nineteen percent of the ORFs on Chromosome 1 code for proteins that are completely unknown.

Forty-two percent of Chromosome 2 ORFs code for known proteins, and 6 percent code for proteins with no known functions. Fifteen percent of Chromosome 2 sequences are similar to those of other ORFs, but products of these genes have not been observed in this microorganism to date. Thirty-eight percent of the ORFs of Chromosome 2 code for completely unknown gene products.

Genes required for growth and viability are mostly located on Chromosome 1, while genes coding for some ribosomal proteins are found on Chromosome 2. Chromosome 2 also codes for some metabolic pathway intermediates. Chromosome 2 has a DNA coding sequence for a segment called an **integron island**. This is a system of proteins that allows the capture of foreign genes. Genes found here include those for drug resistance, for potential virulence genes (hemagglutinin and lipoprotein), and for gene products used by plasmids that allow them to survive in host cells without damage.

Plasmids are extra-chromosomal genetic elements in bacterial cells. In some cases, DNA from the plasmid can become integrated into the DNA of the bacterial cell chromosome. Information on plasmids can give new characteristics to a bacterial cell. These may include drug resistance and enzymes for degradation of certain substances in the environment.

Chromosome 1 contains genes for DNA replication and repair, transcription, translation, cell wall biosynthesis, and a variety of metabolic pathways. Most genes that are known to be required for pathogenesis are located on Chromosome 1. Chromosome 2 contains more genes of unknown function. Many of these genes are located in the integron island of the chromosome.

Researchers have suggested that Chromosome 2 was originally a large plasmid. There are plasmid-type sequences and sequences unlike those from similar bacteria located on Chromosome 2. The integron island located there is similar in sequence to those often found on plasmids. One possibility is that this early plasmid acquired genes from other species but did not integrate those plasmid genes into the DNA of Chromosome 1. Scientists have speculated that uneven segregation at cell division could form cells with Chromosome 2, but not Chromosome 1. Such cells could not replicate, but they could have metabolic activity and be a source of viable cells that cannot be cultured in the laboratory. Such cells might form and survive within biofilms. Genes for regulation pathways are divided about equally between the two chromosomes.

THE RELATIONSHIP BETWEEN THE BACTERIAL VIRUS AND THE GENE FOR CHOLERA TOXIN

Certain viruses, called bacteriophages, infect bacteria and integrate their genetic material into that of the bacterial cell. As the bacterial DNA replicates, the integrated bacteriophage DNA is also copied. On occasion, the virus genome may be excised, or cut out, using enzymes from the bacterial DNA. The bacteriophages may then lyse bacteria that they have infected and reproduced within, so that they can release the new viruses into the environment. This can be induced by some chemicals, temperature changes, or even UV light. Viruses may transfer host DNA from the bacteria it first infected into the DNA of any additional cell that the virus infects. This process, called **transduction**, is one way of exchanging genetic material in bacteria.

The process by which virus DNA is integrated successfully into host bacterial DNA is called lysogeny, and the bacterial viruses engaged in this process are called temperate bacteriophages. If the genes from the bacteriophage introduce genes that give the new recombinant bacterium new characteristics, or phenotypes, this is referred to as lysogenic conversion, since the bacteria have been converted into a new phenotype as a result of infection and lysogeny.

Some bacteriophages are filamentous. Strands of nucleic acid are surrounded by a protein coat. These phages often do not harm the bacterial host and are lysogenic. They may bind to the host at a pilus. One such virus has been found in *Vibrio cholerae*. It is the bacteriophage CTXΦ, which has the genetic code for CT in its genome. This virus uses a special pilus called a toxin-coregulated pilus (TCP) as its receptor on the cholera bacillus, since both the cholera toxin and the pilus are regulated by the same gene (toxR). It was observed that this bacteriophage infects *Vibrio cholerae* more often within the intestinal tract of mice than it does under conditions in the laboratory. Therefore, production of cholera toxin by *Vibrio cholerae* is a result of lysogenic conversion by phage CTXΦ. It is likely that other filamentous phages may also be responsible for transfer of genetic material between different strains of bacteria. (Figure 7.1). In one sense, it may be stated that cholera is caused by a virus!

The genes involved in TCP formation reside on a pathogenicity island on Chromosome 1. This region also codes for

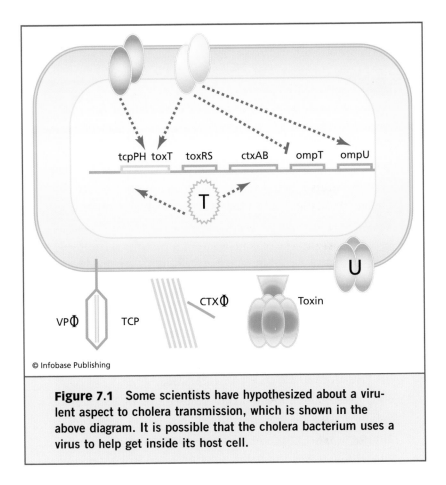

© Infobase Publishing

Figure 7.1 Some scientists have hypothesized about a virulent aspect to cholera transmission, which is shown in the above diagram. It is possible that the cholera bacterium uses a virus to help get inside its host cell.

other genes under control by the toxR regulatory protein and a site for phage integration. This may be the site for integration into the whole chromosome, when this region of DNA was first transferred from another bacterium to the cholera bacillus.

THE LOCATION OF THE GENE FOR CHOLERA TOXIN

The gene for cholera toxin (ctxAB) is located on Chromosome 1 within a genome for a temperate filamentous phage CTXΦ. The gene cluster for the pilus necessary for entry of this filamentous bacteriophage and the regulator gene for toxR, the protein that regulates toxin production, are also located on Chromosome 1.

HORIZONTAL TRANSFER

Horizontal transfer is the process of gene transfer from bacterium to bacterium instead of transfer from bacterium to progeny (vertical transfer). In the example of the cholera bacillus, transfer is mediated by a bacterial virus. This is a source of variability in populations of this pathogenic bacterium. The new strains of cholera that emerged in 1992 resulted after acquisition of new genetic material. This tells us that horizontal gene transfer can create new strains of a pathogen. This could hamper the development of strains for use in **vaccine** preparations as well as in the use of antibiotics. Genes resistant to antibiotics can be transferred in this manner and thus arise in populations rapidly.

ADDITIONAL UNIQUE FEATURES
OF THE *VIBRIO CHOLERAE* GENOME

Both pathogenic and nonpathogenic strains of the cholera bacillus have gene sequences called PilD (also called VcpD). This sequence determines a protein that is required for secretion of CT as well as for the assembly of MSHA (mannose-sensitive hemagglutinin). MSHA is not a virulence factor, but it is important in the formation of biofilms. Biofilms are communities of bacteria in nature, and biofilms containing cholera bacilli have recently been described. The ability of the bacteria to form biofilms is important for the survival of *Vibrio cholerae* in nature. Cholera bacteria live two lifestyles: one in nature and one in a host. The PilD gene connects these lifestyles, and they are equally important for understanding both pathogenesis of the microorganism and its mode of transmission in nature.

Vibrio cholerae has an unusually large number of MCP genes. MCPs are methyl-accepting chemotaxis proteins. These proteins regulate the attraction of the microorganism to sugars, amino acids, oxygen, and other nutrients. **Chemotaxis** is the directed movement of a microorganism toward a particular chemical in its environment. (This is positive chemotaxis; negative chemotaxis is movement away from an area in the environment.) *Escherichia coli* are bacteria that have five MCP genes. *Campylobacterium jejuni,* a pathogen that causes stomach ulcers, has 10 MCP genes. As a result of determining the DNA sequence of the chromosomes of this bacterium, scientists found that *Vibrio cholerae* has 43 MCP genes. These genes are distributed evenly between Chromosome 1 and Chromosome 2. The genes probably arose by gene duplication. The reason(s) for the differences in numbers is presently unclear. One possibility is that each MCP protein in the cholera bacillus is specific for a chemotactic chemical, unlike the MCP proteins of other bacteria, which can sense more than one substrate chemical.

THE COMPLETE DNA SEQUENCE YIELDS NEW INFORMATION

The knowledge of the complete sequence of the nucleic acid bases in the DNA of pathogenic cholera strains of bacteria has given new ways to study this microorganism. Individual genes can be isolated, and the entire genome can be examined to see which genes are needed for infection and survival in the environment and in a host.

One important technique is the formation and use of whole-genome DNA microarrays. This consists of 3,890 pieces of cholera bacterial DNA, each of which represents a known sequence with an ORF. This represents about 93 percent of the entire genome. The polymerase chain reaction (PCR) was used to form sufficient amounts of DNA for each gene segment. These PCR products were spotted onto glass slides coated with polylysine polymer that could bind them. Genomic DNA was purified and fluorescent molecules were attached to it.

Then, fluorescent genomic DNA could be added to the DNA micorarray to find which genomes could bind to the slides. Measuring the fluorescence gave an indication of the amounts of particular genomes found. In this way, scientists could compare different strains of bacteria for different genomes. Also, using variations of this technique, it can be observed when genes are expressed by examining microarrays using whole genomes taken at different times or under different conditions. For example, scientists could ask: Are there genes that are expressed when the microbe is in the intestinal tract that are not expressed when it is found in nature? It will be seen that different genes are expressed at different times in the life cycle of the cholera bacterium.[1, 2]

It was found that *Vibrio cholerae* strains from various pandemics are very similar. Nonpathogenic environmental strains were found to acquire certain genetic segments, probably by horizontal transmission. These include genes coding for neuraminidase enzyme and two regions, VSP-I and VSP-II. These regions contain genes that may be responsible for improving the adaptation of the microbe to aquatic environments, or to better adapt to its human host. This could include resistance of the bacteria to acid in the stomach of the host and improved ability to grow on intestinal cells.

Genome sequencing has been used to find RTX (repeats-in-toxin) genes and genes for new types of pili. These may be important new virulence factors. Genes that form factors that regulate the synthesis of virulence factors such as toxin formation have been discovered. These genes comprise the ToxR regulon, and they may be induced by signals from the environment such as pH, temperature, and ionic strength.[3]

Microarray technology has permitted study of gene expression during infections. Studies to date indicate that during infection, a wide array of specific genes appear. Surprisingly, there is no change in expression of ToxR regulon genes. *Vibrio cholerae* isolated from patient stools are more infectious than bacteria grown in vitro (in culture in a laboratory). Bacteria shed from human patients spread rapidly during outbreaks in contrast to bacteria grown in vitro. These more virulent bacteria have been described as hyperinfectious. This suggests that the genes of unknown function may appear when *V. cholerae* adapts to its host environment.[4]

AUTOINDUCERS

Some bacteria produce and release signal molecules called **autoinducers**. As the population of these bacteria increases, the concentration of these autoinducers also increases. When the concentration reaches a particular level, the bacteria in the population detect these autoinducers and respond by changing their gene expression. In this way, bacteria in populations can communicate. Bacteria with this capability are said to be quorum-sensing.

The autoinducers of *Vibrio cholerae* are called CAI-1, (S)-3 hydroxytridecan-4-1, and AI-2, (2S,4S)-2-methyl-2,3,3,4-tetrahydroxytetrahydrofuran borate. When levels of autoinducers are low (fewer cells present), the protein receptors for the autoinducers are kinases, enzymes that add phosphate to a protein (lux O) that can now activate genes that promote biofilm formation and virulence factor production. As cell density increases, the increase in concentration of autoinducers causes them to bind to their receptors and switch them from kinases to phosphatases. These are enzymes that remove phosphate from lux O and then shut off virulence genes while stabilizing mRNA encoding for the protein HapR. This protein binds to DNA and switches the cell to a high-cell density state. Biofilm and virulence genes are repressed. This likely promotes shedding of cholera bacteria from host to the environment.

It is interesting to note that the presence of the trace element boron as an autoinducer is a rare incidence when a biological function for this chemical is known. This autoinducer is found in luminescent *Vibrio* species as well as in *Vibrio cholerae.* There is an abundance of boron in the oceans where these microorganisms may be found.

BIOFILM AND VIRULENCE GENE CONTROL

Studies of cholera genes have enabled a better understanding of the role of quorum sensing and the regulation of gene expression. Dense pads of cells in biofilms have been related to the survival of a number of pathogens in hosts. Many *Vibrio* species are luminescent *Vibrio* bacteria, and their bioluminescence is regulated by genes that are regulated using quorum sensing. *Vibrio cholerae* is not luminescent, but it has genes similar in sequence to genes for the regulating proteins in their bioluminescent cousins. While researchers were preparing mutants of *V. cholerae*, it was discovered that cholera toxin and TCP production along with genes for membrane transport, secretion, metabolism, chemotaxis, and motility are regulated by quorum sensing. At high cell densities, genes for TCP and CT are repressed while a protease called HAP is induced. In hapR mutants, expression of polysaccharides (vps genes) of *Vibrio* is increased. Without vps genes, biofilm formation is ended. Therefore the HapR gene regulates biofilm formation by signaling it to stop.[5]

In the environment, biofilm formation may enhance the fitness of the bacteria. Polysaccharide production is thought to protect them from the acidic environment of a host (stomach acid). Once in the host, the biofilm may be reduced and the cell density lowered. When the virulence genes are expressed the microbes colonize intestinal sites and form CT. As numbers of bacteria increase, quorum sensing signals repress virulence genes. In these ways, these bacteria are prepared for release from the host and survival in the environment.

Recently, a second system for control of biofilm formation in *Vibrio cholerae* has been described. This is the internal second messenger 3', 5'–cyclic diguanylic acid (c-di-GMP), which

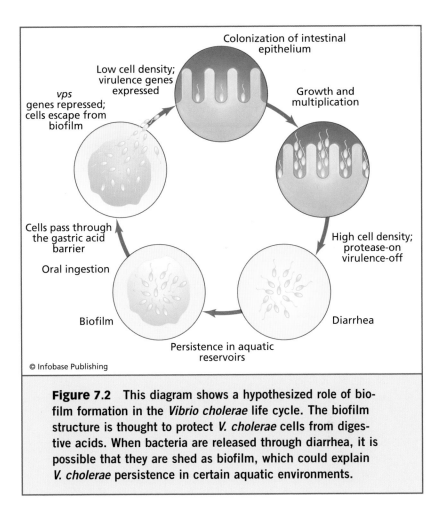

Low cell density;
virulence genes
expressed

vps
genes repressed;
cells escape from
biofilm

Colonization of intestinal
epithelium

Growth and
multiplication

High cell density;
protease-on
virulence-off

Diarrhea

Persistence in aquatic
reservoirs

Biofilm

Oral ingestion

Cells pass through
the gastric acid
barrier

© Infobase Publishing

Figure 7.2   This diagram shows a hypothesized role of biofilm formation in the *Vibrio cholerae* life cycle. The biofilm structure is thought to protect *V. cholerae* cells from digestive acids. When bacteria are released through diarrhea, it is possible that they are shed as biofilm, which could explain *V. cholerae* persistence in certain aquatic environments.

activates biofilm formation. HapR binds to and represses the expression of the vps activator for biofilm formation. In addition, HapR controls proteins that synthesize and degrade c-di-GMP. At high cell density, cellular levels of c-di-GMP are reduced and biofilm formation is decreased.

Biofilm formation permits *Vibrio cholerae* to survive in a low-nutrient environment and to increase its infectivity. Once bacteria colonize the host, its biofilms disperse.

Having these two systems to control biofilm and virulence formation gives *Vibrio cholerae* an incredible flexibility to live in two very different worlds. Itemizing all of the genes in *V. cholerae* has enabled scientists to discover when and where certain genes are expressed in understanding the adaptations to these two environments.[6]

8

Treatments for Cholera

In 1849, a cholera outbreak killed 10 percent of the population of St. Louis, Missouri. More than half of those suffering from the disease died from severe diarrhea and fluid loss. In comparison, when cholera attacked more than 300,000 people in Peru in 1991, fewer than 1 percent of the infected people died. Although these people also developed the severe diarrhea that accompanies this infection, there were treatments available to replace lost body fluids, which in turn saved many lives. The death rate among untreated cases is typically about 50 percent.

In spite of the vast improvements in our understanding of the molecular mechanisms of cholera virulence, and the adaptation of the cholera bacillus to life in two different environments, the major breakthrough in treatment once infection occurs remains fluid replacement.

IMPROVED TREATMENT—IMPROVED CRISIS MANAGEMENT

As understanding of the bacillus has improved over the years, with it has come improved ways to treat infected individuals. Even before the cholera bacillus was discovered by Koch and was shown to be the cause of this disease, physicians recognized the importance of replacing fluids lost from the body as a result of severe diarrhea. Today, replacing fluids, as well as the important electrolytes, the ions dissolved in the liquids, remains the key to the treatment of cholera. At first **fluid replacement therapy**, which replaces lost body fluids, was performed by giving patients **hypertonic** (as opposed to **hypotonic**) solutions containing a higher amount of electrolytes **intravenously**. The mortality rates of cholera patients who received fluid replacement therapy dropped about 30 percent compared to those who were untreated.

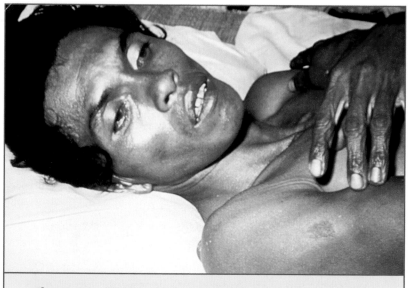

Figure 8.1 "Folded skin" often results from extreme loss of fluids associated with cholera. Extreme dehydration causes skin to lose its elasticity. (Courtesy CDC)

ADDITIONAL STEPS IN THE TREATMENT OF CHOLERA

Step 1: Fluid replacement
Step 2: Maintain the level of fluids in the patient
Step 3: Treatment with antibiotics
Step 4: Adequate nutrition

FLUID REPLACEMENT

In the 1960s, scientists discovered that the transport of sodium and water was facilitated by the presence of glucose. This led to a simple, practical, safe, inexpensive, and effective way to treat cholera, called **ORT** (oral rehydration therapy). ORT is an important and valuable medical tool for treating diarrheal diseases, including cholera.

The World Health Organization (WHO) recommends a solution for ORT that contains: sodium chloride (90 mmol/liter), potassium chloride (20 mmol/liter), glucose (111 mmol/liter), and sodium bicarbonate (30 mmol/liter) or sodium citrate (10 mmol/liter). This supplies the appropriate replacement of lost electrolytes as well as a correct pH level. These solutions are provided in sterile ORS (oral replacement solutions) packets. In emerging nations, such packets or other sources of sterile ORS may not be readily available. However, an emergency solution can be prepared using 3.5 grams of sodium chloride (about 1/2 teaspoon of table salt) and 20 grams (about 2 tablespoons) of sugar mixed into a liter of water. These solutions have saved numerous lives and have halted epidemics.

Along with electrolytes, cholera patients will lose bicarbonate in their stools. Therefore, it is necessary to also supply an alkaline solution to replace lost bicarbonate. Originally, sodium bicarbonate was used. However, bicarbonate solutions do not keep for long periods of time, particularly if stored in hot and humid tropical climates. Sodium citrate has been found to be an excellent substitute. Scientists have compared oral replacement solutions with bicarbonate and citrate, and found them to be equally effective.

Oral rehydration solutions prepared with sucrose, which is more readily available than glucose, were also tested. Sucrose is broken down by enzymes in the intestine to form both fructose and glucose. However, these enzymes may not be sufficiently active when the patient has severe diarrhea. Comparison studies have shown that ORS-glucose therapy is slightly more effective than ORS-sucrose therapy.

RECENT IMPROVEMENTS OF
FLUID REPLACEMENT THERAPIES

Another approach to ORT has been to prepare solutions in which glucose is replaced by starches and proteins common to the patient's diet. The idea is that starches and proteins will be digested in the intestine, releasing glucose, amino acids, and peptides. These are all organic chemicals that should help the uptake of sodium and water. Cereals, especially rice, are commonly used and should also supply nutrients without an additional loss of fluids.

It was shown that rice powder ORS (30 grams of rice powder per liter) was as effective as sucrose ORS. A reduction of diarrheal output can also be accomplished with this formulation. Other grains that have been used successfully are from wheat and maize. Unlike rice powder, the wheat preparation does not have to be cooked. These formulations are very useful and, depending on local conditions, may be used in place of glucose ORT.

At the present, there is still a need to reduce the volume output of diarrhea caused by cholera. Some of the current efforts to improve ORS formulations include the substitution of organic acids other than citrate, the use of polymers of glucose, and the use of amino acids. Some of these formulations seem promising in clinical trials, but the best ORT is the cereal-based formulations.

In emergency situations, "sugar-salt" solutions can be easily prepared from commonly available materials to use in therapy. However, this solution has no base (bicarbonate) or potassium. A diet supplement of foods rich in potassium is recommended in these cases. These solutions are incomplete and should be used as temporary measures for treatment only.

CHOLERA OUTBREAKS

The World Health Organization estimates that there are about 100,000 cases of cholera each year. There were 131,943 reported cases in 2005. This is most likely an underestimate, since many victims without access to medical care go unreported.

This fact is all the more remarkable when one realizes that cholera is an infectious disease that can be prevented.

Source: World Health Organization

Recently, the formulation of ORS has been changed. The recommended concentration of sodium has been lowered to 75 mmol/liter. Concentrations of sodium that are any lower than this can lead to sodium deficiency, but this is a preferred concentration. Some patients may have difficulty consuming adequate fluids or may vomit, preventing sufficient intake. In such cases, fluids are given intravenously.

PROPER CARE FOR THE PATIENT

Health care workers should evaluate cholera patients carefully in order to be able to determine the proper treatment. For example, caregivers must know how much fluid the patient has lost in order to determine how much needs to be replaced. Patients should also be examined for pulse rate, skin turgor, nausea and vomiting, fullness of neck veins, and weight loss.

For patients with severe diarrhea, IV-ORT (intravenous oral replacement therapy) is preferable. Severely dehydrated patients can be rehydrated in two to four hours. The degree of dehydration in the patient determines the best rehydration therapy to use. Dehydration is rated by clinicians in four groups: (1) no dehydration, (2) mild, (3) moderate, and (4) severe dehydration. The mild category patient has lost about 5 percent of his or her body weight in fluid and may have somewhat reduced skin turgor. The moderately dehydrated patient has lost 7.5 percent of body weight, has poor skin turgor, a dry mouth, and somewhat sunken eyes. Patients who have lost 10 percent or more body weight are weak and lethargic, have very poor skin turgor and very sunken eyes, and have rapid, thready pulse rates. They are considered severely dehydrated.

The weight of the patient should be noted upon admission for treatment so that weight gain from rehydration therapy can be observed. Weight can also be used to estimate the percent of dehydration. For example, an individual weighing 50 kg (110 lbs) and who suffers from severe dehydration, will require about five liters of fluid to replace fluid loss (50 kg x 10% = 5 kg). A child weighing 10 kg (22 lbs) with mild dehydration would require 500 ml (17 oz) of replacement fluid.

STABILIZING THE PATIENT

Once fluid replacement therapy has stabilized a patient, it is necessary to make sure no more fluid is lost until diarrhea ceases. This is called **maintenance therapy**. A specially designed cot, called a **cholera cot** (Figure 8.2), may be used for this purpose. This cot has a plastic sheet under the patient. There is an opening in the cot through which the plastic sheet directs fluids lost from diarrhea to empty into a container placed below the cot. This container is calibrated so that an attendant can record the amount of fluid lost. This will provide the information needed so that the caregiver can give enough fluid to the patient to maintain proper hydration levels. A container for vomit is also provided, as patients lose fluid this way, too. The cholera cot provides the information needed to keep the patient stabilized until the infection begins to wane.

THE USE OF ANTIBIOTICS

Patients who are seriously ill with cholera should be given a 1 to 3 day course of **antibiotic** therapy. This will shorten the illness and reduce loss of fluids. The antibiotic of choice in most cases is 300 mg of doxycycline given in a single dose. Antibiotic therapy should begin from three to six hours after the start of fluid replacement therapy. Combining rehydration therapy with antibiotics means that the patient's hospital stay will be shortened, and he or she will require less rehydration fluids. This treatment course can be beneficial in areas where intravenous fluids and other supplies are limited.

Samples of bacteria should be taken from a select number of patients during an outbreak. These should be screened for antibiotic sensitivity to identify the particular strain of this outbreak. If the strains isolated are found to be resistant to tetracyclines (such as doxycycline), other antibiotics are used.

Figure 8.2 Cholera cots are specially designed so that caregivers can carefully monitor the amount of fluid a patient loses through the course of the disease. The cot contains a plastic sheet with a hole in the middle, which directs diarrhea to a bucket beneath the bed. This allows the caregiver to determine how much rehydration therapy is necessary to stabilize the patient. (© Georges Gobet/AFP/Getty Images)

These include erythromycin, co-trimoxazole, ciprofloxacin, and azithromycin. Antibiotics should not be administered to mild cases or as a preventative. Overuse of antibiotics increases the risk that strains of cholera with antibiotic resistance will develop.

There are problems with the use of antibiotics. People tend to expect antibiotics to be a permanent cure in all cases of infection. This is not the case for cholera. Antibiotics are expensive and may not be practical in poor nations. Antibiotics may also have side effects in many cases. These side effects may come at a time when the health of the patient is already

Table 8.1 Antibiotics Used to Treat Cholera

Antibiotic	Treatment Course	Children[1]	Adults
Doxycycline	Single dose	n/a	300 mg[2]
Tetracycline	4 times per day for 3 days	12.5 mg/kg	500 mg
Trimethoprim/ sulfamethoxazole	2 times per day for 3 days	TMP 5 mg/kg and SMX 25 mg/kg[3]	TMP 160 mg and SMX 800 mg
Furazolidone	4 times per day for 3 days	1.25 mg/kg	100 mg[4]

[1] Children's doses are determined by the child's weight.
[2] Antibiotic of choice for adults (except for pregnant women) because only one dose is required.
[3] This is the recommended drug course for children.
[4] This is the antibiotic of choice for pregnant women.

Source: WHO's guidelines for treating cholera

compromised. Use of antibiotics may help only a few, and it may prolong the time in which those that have been treated can still become infected with the cholera bacillus. Since the benefits of antibiotic therapy are limited, their routine use is not recommended. However, use after maintenance therapy can hasten the healing process.

A major public health problem is antibiotic resistance, particularly because this resistance is often multiple resistance. Resistance to one antibiotic might mean that the microorganism is resistant to several other, different antibiotics. In 1977, multiple antibiotic resistant *Vibrio cholerae* O1 (MARV) appeared in Tanzania, and then in Bangladesh. These strains carried a piece of DNA that could integrate into the bacterial chromosome and was easily transmitted to nonresistant bacteria. This was called an SXT element, and its presence gave the bacteria resistance to sulfamethoxazole, trimethoprim, chloramphenicol, and streptomycin.

Antibiotic resistance has appeared as a result of a variety of different mutations. For example, fluoroquinolines have excellent activity against *V. cholerae*. Strains resistant to this and other related quinoline antibiotics have appeared. Mutations giving strains the ability to pump out the antibiotic as fast as it may enter have been described.

An example of this was experienced in 1998. Up to that time, the Indian Ocean had been free of cholera for years. Then, in January 1998, an outbreak of cholera occurred. One coastal city and another province were surrounded by a sanitary barricade. All individuals leaving these areas were routinely given oral doxycycline (an antibiotic). Patients with severe diarrhea were also given the same antibiotic. In spite of this, cholera reached all 10 provinces on the Comoros Islands within 10 months. A surveillance team was established, and they found that the strain of *Vibrio cholerae* there was serogroup O1, serotype Ogawa, biotype El Tor. It was resistant to trimethoprim-sulfamethoxazole, sulfonamides, trimethoprim, chloramphenicol, and streptomycin as well as agent 0129, a naturally occurring chemical that normally kills cholera bacteria. Of all the strains of cholera bacilli isolated, 55 percent were found to be resistant to tetracycline as well as the antibiotics listed above. This pattern continued as other strains were isolated at other locations on the islands.

The proportions of isolated bacteria that were resistant to tetracycline continued to climb. Therefore, authorities recommended that doctors and public health officials 1) not routinely use antibiotics for cholera prevention, 2) use oral rehydration therapy for mild-to-moderate cases, and 3) use antibiotics for cases of severe cholera illnesses only. They also recommended that the areas should be continually monitored for antibiotic-resistant strains, so that emergency antibiotic therapy could be used properly when needed.

Other studies have shown that the resistance genes in cholera are carried on **conjugative plasmids**, which are plasmids needed for bacteria to mate by a process called **conjugation**, bearing multiple resistance gene locations. Bacterial viruses that kill cholera bacilli have been tried as therapy. This was found not to be as useful as tetracycline treatment.

Efforts to discover new antibiotic therapies continue. In 2004 researchers from the University of New South Wales in Australia isolated compounds from the seaweed *Delisea pulchra* that block the quorum-sensing interaction between cholera, and perhaps other, bacteria. These compounds, furanones, prevent bacteria from switching on virulence mechanisms. To date, these have not been used clinically, but this research offers a new approach to developing antibiotics to fight bacteria dependent on quorum-sensing mechanisms to turn on their virulence genes.

In 2006 a report in the *New England Journal of Medicine* described a single-dose treatment for cholera in adults using the antibiotic azithromycin. Within 48 hours of treatment, 73 percent of patients stopped having watery diarrhea. By comparison, 27 percent of patients who had been treated with ciprofloxacin stopped having diarrhea. Further, 78 percent of patients receiving azithromycin were free of infecting bacteria as compared to 10 percent treated with ciprofloxacin. This new treatment would reduce costly hospital stays, and it costs less than $1 per dose. Yet the use of antibiotic therapy remains controversial.

In the same issue of the *New England Journal of Medicine*, Dr. Richard Guerrat described "two troubling lessons" from these findings. First, the use of antibiotics will undoubtedly be met with the development of resistant strains. Secondly, he pointed out that there has been a failure to have a sanitary revolution throughout the world. Such a revolution occurred in North America and Europe over 100 years ago, but it has not occurred worldwide. Guerrat describes an incident from February 1992, when 75 patients with severe diarrhea from cholera arrived in Los Angeles from Peru. They had eaten cholera-contaminated cold seafood salad on the plane. Ten were hospitalized and one person died. There was not a single case of someone acquiring cholera from these patients. Once clean water and sanitation were provided, there was no spread of the cholera microorganism. This pointed out to Guerrat that access to clean water and sanitation are more important in the long run than the use of antimicrobial agents.[1, 2]

THE ROLE OF NUTRITION

The cholera patient should be given nutritious, age-appropriate food, even before the diarrhea stops. This is the final stage of treatment, and this helps the patient return to health.

Finally, scientists are attempting to develop specific medications to reduce the debilitating diarrhea. They have found that chlorpromazine and nicotinic acid are useful in this regard. However, research is still in the early stages, and the mode of action of the drugs and patient responses have not been studied thoroughly. While there will always be searches for better ways of treatment, the methods described in this chapter are the best and most widely used at present.

9
Prevention

CLEAN WATER—THE BEST PREVENTION

People who reside in developed nations often take clean water for granted. Yet, clean water and modern sewage treatment facilities are the main reasons that cholera is no longer a problem in nations that can afford to maintain sanitary conditions. In the United States and other nations, cholera increased as the growth of population centers increased. Even before cholera and other infectious diseases were shown to be associated with contaminated water supplies, many cities developed ways to provide clean water and sewage treatment facilities.

Modern and well-maintained water treatment facilities and sewage treatment plants are the best prevention against cholera outbreaks. Where such facilities do not exist, as in many underdeveloped nations, waterborne infectious diseases cause problems. It is for this reason that cholera is often referred to as a disease of the poor.

Crowded cities and international travel provide other conditions for the spread of cholera. In the United States and other developed nations, there are public health agencies that oversee the maintenance of clean water and sewage treatment facilities. When a cholera case appears in the United States, determination and prompt action by public health personnel, elimination of the sources of infection, and sanitation will prevent an outbreak. This includes the proper disposal of fecal waste to halt transmission of the disease.

PREVENTION WITHOUT CLEAN WATER FACILITIES

Where there are no clean water facilities, careful food and water handling and prompt medical treatment can prevent and reduce the incidence of cholera. Boiling water, for example, will kill the cholera bacillus. However, it is not always easy or practical to sustain the boiling of all water supplies. Water is often stored in homes in poorer nations, and it may be dipped out by hand. Thus the water may be contaminated. One simple solution to this practice has been to use water containers with narrow-mouthed openings. These require pouring rather than hand scooping the water. Other efforts are the addition of chlorine to disinfect the water supply. Likewise, better attention to the production of safe ice supplies is important, and this should also be monitored.

Individuals can protect themselves by thoroughly cooking food before eating it. Often, street vendors sell foods such as shellfish, which may have been caught in unsafe waters and may therefore be contaminated with cholera bacilli. Providing cleaner vending carts and the means for their sanitation would be beneficial. All of these methods require the education of people in areas prone to cholera epidemics. Even then, the cholera bacillus requires few lapses in these routine types of sanitation procedures in order for it to start another round of infections.

Once it was clearly established that *Vibrio cholerae* is commensal with organisms in the zooplankton of oceans, especially with copepods, a new strategy was developed to significantly reduce the numbers of these bacteria in water. *Vibrio cholerae* has been shown to exist in the copepod gut, surfaces, egg cases, and oral regions. These copepods in plankton are important for the survival, multiplication, and transmission of cholera.

In many rural villages it is too costly to use firewood to boil water supplies. Cloth from saris has been used in rural Bangladesh to filter home-prepared drinks. Filtering water with sari cloth is an inexpensive and culturally acceptable way to reduce the numbers of cholera bacteria in water supplies. This method has been tested for its ability to remove copepods and has been shown to reduce the occurrence of cholera by half.

The cloth traps the copepods but not free-swimming bacteria. The method is able to reduce the numbers of bacteria significantly. Less expensive cloth filters work as well as more expensive nylon cloth, too. Used sari cloth is preferable to new cloth for the filtration. Electron microscopy shows that sari cloth folded four to eight times creates a filter with a pore size about 20 μm. This is adequate to remove copepods and the bacteria attached to them. Often this is sufficient to reduce the numbers of bacteria in water to levels below the infectious dose.[1]

ADDITIONAL PRECAUTIONS

Should antibiotics be used as a **prophylactic** measure? Studies of preventative treatments in which family members of cholera patients are given antibiotics (20 doses of tetracycline over a five-day period) show that there is a 13 percent decrease in the incidence of infection among family members. This kind of treatment may be valuable in isolated environments, such as on ships, where the infection might be contained. However, antibiotic prophylaxis will not control cholera in open environments. In addition, strains with antibiotic resistance appear when there is widespread use of antibiotic therapy. This resistance is often to multiple drug, and thus reduces the number and different kinds of antibiotics that can be used to treat infections. The use of antibiotics may also lead many people to let down their guard, wanting to believe that the antibiotic treatment is a permanent cure for the infection. They may practice good sanitation less stringently. Antibiotic treatment is not a cure and is not without side effects in many cases.

IS THERE A PERMANENT CURE FOR CHOLERA?

Vaccination is the practice of introducing a foreign substance into an organism to elicit an immune response, ideally in order to obtain permanent, or at least long-lasting, protection from the foreign agent. Vaccination against the smallpox virus was demonstrated by previous exposure to cowpox, which is closely related to the human virus.

Figure 9.1 This woman in Bangladesh (right) is using sari cloth as a filter as she collects drinking water. This filtration method removes cholera-carrying copepods from the water, greatly reducing the spread of the disease in poor areas where disinfectants and fuel for boiling water are limited. (Courtesy of Anwar Huq, Maryland Pathogen Research Institute, University of Maryland, College Park, Maryland)

When microorganisms were identified as the causes of many infectious diseases, scientists immediately tried to make preparations of the infectious agent that would give immunity while not infecting an individual. The trick is to modify the infecting agent in such a way that it can call up a strong immune response in an individual while not causing the disease. To that end, scientists tried a number of ways to modify or **attenuate** infectious bacteria. One attempt to prepare such an attenuated form of the cholera bacillus was prepared and used as a vaccine the year after Koch identified the cholera bacillus. However, this

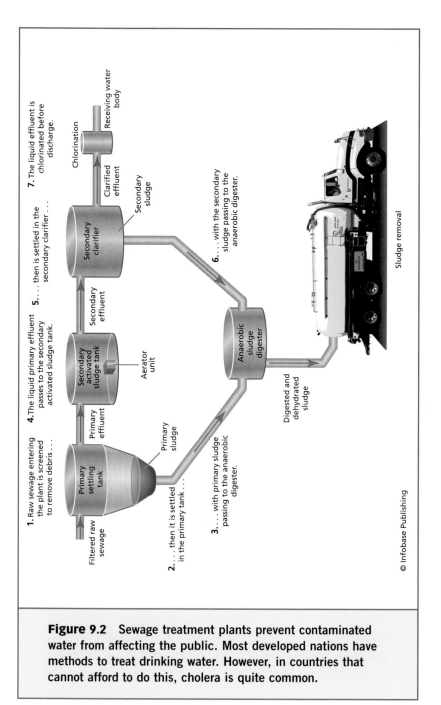

1. Raw sewage entering the plant is screened to remove debris . . .

Filtered raw sewage

Primary settling tank

2. . . . then it is settled in the primary tank . . .

Primary sludge

Primary effluent

3. . . . with primary sludge passing to the anaerobic digester.

4. The liquid primary effluent passes to the secondary activated sludge tank.

Secondary activated sludge tank

Aerator unit

Secondary effluent

5. . . . then is settled in the secondary clarifier . . .

Secondary clarifier

Clarified effluent

Secondary sludge

Chlorination

7. The liquid effluent is chlorinated before discharge.

Receiving water body

6. . . . with the secondary sludge passing to the anaerobic digester.

Anaerobic sludge digester

Digested and dehydrated sludge

Sludge removal

© Infobase Publishing

Figure 9.2 Sewage treatment plants prevent contaminated water from affecting the public. Most developed nations have methods to treat drinking water. However, in countries that cannot afford to do this, cholera is quite common.

vaccine was not successful since many people who received the inoculation had a variety of side effects. Scientists suspect that these "attenuated bacterial preparations" contained microorganisms other than cholera bacilli.

Louis Pasteur thought that live microorganisms made the best vaccines. He encouraged a colleague to develop such a live vaccine. It had been observed that once someone survived a cholera infection, he or she was immune to reinfection. One of Pasteur's colleagues attenuated cholera bacteria by growing it at 102.2°F (39°C) with oxygen aeration. He also prepared a more highly infectious strain by passing it repeatedly through guinea pigs. The microbe would be injected into the animals, then isolated, and then injected into other animals. In this way, a more infectious strain was selected. He injected the attenuated preparation and after a short wait, challenged the immunity of the "vaccinated" individuals who had received the attenuated bacteria by giving them a dose of the more infectious bacteria. The results were not promising because the volunteers developed many side effects. In other words, they were sicker from the vaccination than from the disease!

In 1893, Russian bacteriologist Waldemar Haffkine developed a whole-cell injectable cholera vaccine in India. It was widely used through the 1950s. It provided 48 percent protection for at least three months. Frequent booster injections were required, however, and there were frequent side effects.

Other investigators tried preparing vaccines by growing cholera bacilli on agar and then heating them so that they were no longer alive. This process is called heat inactivation and is often used to attenuate bacteria. This vaccine was first tried in Japan in 1902 with limited success. Still other researchers attempted to inactivate the cholera bacillus using bile. These preparations were called bilivaccines. When used in tablet form they provided protection for 82 percent of a population. However, this method failed because of reactions to the bile in the preparations.

It was not until the 1960s that interest was revived in the preparation of a cholera vaccine. Investigators tried using whole bacterial cells as well as the cholera toxin or components of the toxin for vaccine preparations. Strain JBK 70, deficient in both the A and B toxin subunits (tox^{A-} tox^{B-}), induced the formation of antibodies that kill cholera bacilli and for this reason are called vibriocidal antibodies. Preparations using whole toxins or toxin B subunit induced antitoxin in the serum, but it did not last very long. Such preparations were found to induce a secretion of antibodies from intestinal cells. This meant that both whole cells and toxin preparations would be needed for an effective vaccine. Presumably, the antitoxin formed from intestinal cells prevents binding of the bacillus. The role of the vibriocidal antibodies in protection is less clear, since the microbes are rarely found in the bloodstream. Vaccines containing the B subunit of the toxin as well as whole attenuated *Vibrio cholera* cells that have been made ineffective give good protection. This preparation is given orally. Such a preparation is referred to as **synergistic**, since two preparations (the whole bacterium and the toxin-derived antigen, which induces antibody formation) give better protection together than each does when used alone.

The vibriocidal antibody induced by the vaccine for the most part reacts against the lipopolysaccharide antigen. Since both the toxin subunit proteins and the proteins for the structure of pili are controlled by the same regulatory protein (TCP-toxic co-regulated pilus), it is thought that the antibody formed in reaction to the toxin subunits prevents attachment by the pili.

METHODS AND APPROACHES TO VACCINE PREPARATION

Vaccines can be prepared from dead whole cells. They may be prepared from one strain (**monovalent**) or from more than one strain (**polyvalent**). Vaccines can also be prepared from fragments of cells, such as protein subunits of a toxin or outer membrane preparations rich in lipopolysaccharides. Toxins can be modified by physical or chemical treatments to remain antigenic without being toxic. These are called **toxoids**. Cells may be attenuated in more traditional methods, such as treatment with aldehydes (like formaldehyde or glutaraldehyde), alcohol, and/or heat. Mutant strains of pathogenic microorganisms lacking genes to determine known virulence factors can also be prepared. These should remain antigenic, while also remaining nontoxic. More recently, **recombinant DNA** technologies have been used to prepare such modified strains.

APPROACHES TO CHOLERA VACCINE PREPARATION

Vaccines with dead whole cells give some protection. A polyvalent preparation for cholera was effective in a little more than half of the cases. Preparations of outer membranes given orally gave a good response but were not well studied in field tests. Toxoid vaccines did not provide significant protection. B toxin subunit preparations were capable of inducing significant antibody response, but the effectiveness as a vaccine alone was not studied thoroughly. Combination oral vaccines were prepared from different sources. One, a preparation of multivalent dead whole cells added to a purified B toxin protein subunit, was shown to be the best. It was effective more than 60 percent of the time.

At first, scientists attempted to use nontoxic strains in vaccines. However, naturally occurring and chemically induced mutant strains that lacked virulence components proved disappointing. One, a strain called Texas Star-SR, lacked the ability to synthesize the A toxin subunit but could synthesize the B subunit. It was discovered by screening mutants induced by nitrosoguanidine, a **mutagen**. While this strain was promising, the possibility of reversion of the induced and unknown mutations was a drawback. Scientists needed to look for more precise methods for preparing mutants.

New methods emerged with the advent of recombinant DNA technology. With these techniques, scientists can delete specific genes that determine the virulence properties of certain cells. They can also isolate strains that cannot grow in the intestine. The virulence genes can be removed from cholera bacilli and placed into bacteria that are otherwise rendered harmless. However, these approaches have been somewhat disappointing. For example, genetically engineered strains that cannot form either the A or B subunits of the cholera toxin, and strains that cannot form A but can form the B subunit of the toxin, were prepared. Both induced loose stools in a significant number of cases. The strain producing the B subunit also produced a hemolysin. The role of this in pathogenicity is unknown. Scientists created a new strain, which they labeled CVD 103. It is A^-B^+ but also lacks TCP, a colonization factor for pili attachment to intestinal cells. Further, this strain was made resistant to mercury (Hg^{++}), so that it can easily be distinguished from a wild type strain of *Vibrio cholerae* O1. There was mild diarrhea in 2 percent of the cases tested, and there was a significant increase in vibriocidal antibodies in cases vaccinated using this strain.

CURRENT VACCINES

WHO currently recommends the inactivated vaccine Dukoral, licensed by SBL Vaccine, Sweden. This is composed of heat- or formalin-killed whole cell *Vibrio cholerae* O1, serotypes Inaba and Ogawa, and classic and El Tor biotypes. In addition, these four preparations are supplemented with purified cholera toxin B subunit (CTB). This whole cell/recombinant subunit (WC/rBS) vaccine is given orally with a buffer that serves to neutralize normal acidity of the stomach.

In field trials in Peru and Bangladesh, there was 80 to 90 percent protection during six months in all age groups. Two doses were given one to two weeks apart. The protection declined in young children after six months but remained at about 60 percent after two years in older children and adults.

In Vietnam, a vaccine similar to the Dukoral vaccine has been developed. It contains no recombinant CTB subunit. It remains 66 percent effective against *Vibrio cholerae* El Tor after eight months in all age groups. The vaccine is available and used in Vietnam. Recently, a whole cell oral vaccine using O1 and O139 strains has been developed. It is safe and immunogenic in both children and adults. There is 90 percent protection against strain O1 and 68 percent protection against strain O139. This vaccine offers promise and is being tested in other countries.

The other major vaccine in use is a live, attenuated vaccine developed using *Vibrio cholerae* O1 Inaba strain (CVD103-HgR) that has been genetically modified to produce CTB but not the A subunit of cholera toxin. This vaccine is called Orochal and is licensed to Berna Biotech, Switzerland. It is given orally with neutralizing buffer. There are two forms available: a low dose type for nonendemic countries and a tenfold higher dose for countries where cholera is endemic. It was found to be 80 percent protective against all *V. cholerae* after testing it on volunteers with *Vibrio cholerae* O1 (either classical or El Tor biotype). When tested in Indonesia, a cholera endemic nation, there were limited cases of cholera at the time, so the vaccine was not shown to demonstrate protection. However, a later field test in Micronesia suggests a positive result, giving protection against cholera in an endemic area during an epidemic.

Other vaccines are being prepared and tested. In Malaysia, a vaccine using purified naked cholera DNA is being developed. A cholera vaccine has also been prepared in rice plants. To date, however, WHO recommends the use of killed oral WC/rBS vaccine as a way to prevent cholera during epidemics.[2]

RICE VACCINE

A novel means to produce and deliver a cholera vaccine was developed at the University of Tokyo in 2007. Immunologists inserted genetic material from *Vibrio cholerae* into the genome of rice plants. The material inserted determined the cholera toxin B (CTB) subunit. It was found that an average of 30 micrograms of CTB was expressed in each rice grain.

When consumed, the rice seeds expressing CTB were recognized by cells of the immune system that are in the gut. These M cells then formed CTB-specific antibodies that could neutralize cholera toxin. This is a mucosal response, the formation of antibodies at the intestinal mucosa, where initial infection with cholera occurs.

Inside the seed, CTB is stored in protein bodies. The CTB is not degraded by the enzyme pepsin, even though other proteins in the seed are destroyed by this digestive enzyme. Therefore, this vaccine resists the harsh chemical environment in the gastrointestinal tract. The seeds can be stored at room temperature for more than 15 years, and the CTB remains stable and immunologically potent during this time.

The vaccine will not be delivered as steamed rice. It is likely that a tablet or capsule made with rice-based vaccine will be developed. It may be necessary to take periodic booster doses to keep the immune system updated. This technology is an exciting discovery that promises a low-cost, effective, and practical regimen to control cholera and, perhaps in the future, other infectious diseases.[3,4]

HERD IMMUNITY

If a certain percentage of a population is rendered immune to an infectious disease, the transmission of the infection can be reduced significantly. This observation describes herd immunity. One study has developed a model that shows that in a population in which 50 percent received an oral vaccine, then 93 percent of the overall population would be protected. Little is known about possible synergistic effects of different means of preventing cholera. It seems likely that vaccination combined with use of recommended control measures gives promise to control or prevent future cholera outbreaks. As none of the described vaccines is 100 percent effective, sanitation remains key to controlling exposures and disease outbreaks.

VACCINATIONS IN THE UNITED STATES

In the United States, the Public Health Service does not require vaccination for travelers coming to the United States from cholera-infected areas. The World Health Organization does not recommend cholera vaccination for travel to or from cholera-infected regions. Vaccines present in the United States are prepared from a combination of phenol-inactivated suspensions of Inaba and Ogawa classic strains grown on agar or in broth. High-risk personnel should be vaccinated, however, including at least one booster shot within six months of the first shot. There is no general recommendation for United States citizens or residents.

SHOULD WE BE CONCERNED?

We should be concerned about the welfare of others and about the possibilities of new cholera strains reaching the United States. An effective vaccine will help thousands around the world, a world now made smaller because of rapid international travel.

10

Cholera Today

Pathogenic *Vibrio cholerae* live in two very different worlds: the ocean environment and the human environment. Using a wide variety of approaches to study this microorganism, scientists have explored this microbe on the molecular, cellular, and environmental levels. These studies have involved genetics, epidemiology, remote sensing, and computer technologies. The result is an understanding of the extraordinary adaptability of this microorganism.

In an aqueous environment, *Vibrios* may be free swimming or may attach to various life forms such as copepods and blue crabs. In these environments, the microbe has receptor sites for attaching to chitin, the hard exoskeleton of these aquatic life forms, or to the cells of the hindgut and oral regions of these hosts. They may enter a noncultivatable or dormant-like state. They form biofilms that may promote their survival.

As free-swimming *Vibrios*, these bacteria are capable of exchanging genetic material that can help them adapt to changing environments. This occurred recently with the appearance of an O1, O139 strain from a non-O1, O139 strain and the regular appearance of antibiotic resistant strains.

Once consumed by a human, the microbe enters a completely different environment. Quorum-sensing control systems facilitate this adaptation. The microbe must now adapt to life at a more acidic pH. Once past that barrier, the microbes possess receptor sites to attach to microvilli in the epithelium of the gut. Here they proliferate and secrete cholera toxin. This leads to diarrhea and possible epidemic spread of the disease. Now discharged into the environment, the bacteria must adapt again to life on

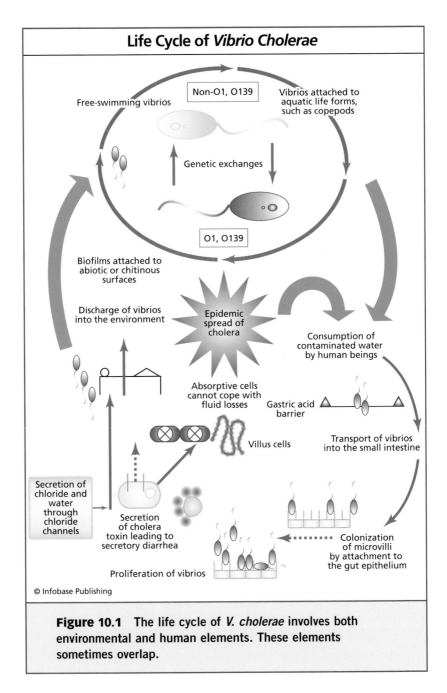

Life Cycle of *Vibrio Cholerae*

Free-swimming vibrios

Non-O1, O139

Vibrios attached to aquatic life forms, such as copepods

Genetic exchanges

O1, O139

Biofilms attached to abiotic or chitinous surfaces

Discharge of vibrios into the environment

Epidemic spread of cholera

Consumption of contaminated water by human beings

Absorptive cells cannot cope with fluid losses

Gastric acid barrier

Villus cells

Transport of vibrios into the small intestine

Secretion of chloride and water through chloride channels

Secretion of cholera toxin leading to secretory diarrhea

Colonization of microvilli by attachment to the gut epithelium

Proliferation of vibrios

© Infobase Publishing

Figure 10.1 The life cycle of *V. cholerae* involves both environmental and human elements. These elements sometimes overlap.

the outside, completing this cycle through two very different worlds.

MODERN INTERVENTIONS

Just as there are a number of ways that changes can alter the patterns of cholera outbreaks, there are a number of different approaches to interrupt the life cycle of this microorganism and reduce or eliminate outbreaks.

Observing diagrams of the life cycle of *Vibrio cholerae* shows the places where changes in these patterns of growth can happen. Changes in climate, including variation in the bacterial population, can result in genetic exchanges. Changes in the water supply, including its treatment, occur. The general health of potential human hosts can vary.

By understanding this, modern approaches to prevention of cholera have become multifaceted. First, scientists can predict cholera epidemics by monitoring algal blooms, particularly in endemic areas. Providing a clean water supply, one of the oldest interventions, is still the best way to prevent cholera. Where modern water treatment facilities are not available, simple filtration with cloth can help reduce the numbers of bacteria in water. If the bacteria find their way into a human host, medical interventions may include antibiotic therapy, fluid replacement, and vaccination.

IS CHOLERA AN EMERGING INFECTIOUS DISEASE?

An **emerging infectious disease** is one that is newly recognized, often as a result of human activity. The microorganisms in question may have been around for thousands of years without causing health problems but may have recently infected humans. A classic example of an emerging disease is the microbe *Legionella pneumophila,* which causes Legionnaire's disease (a type of pneumonia) after it is inhaled. This microbe was originally found in soil, where it is generally harmless. However, air conditioners with holding tanks that opened into the outside environment (as opposed to fully enclosed holding tanks) increased in usage by the 1970s. *Legionella pneumophila* microbes thrived in the holding tanks and could be spread to humans by droplets. Human beings had created the mechanism and opportunity for an increase in infections caused by this microorganism.

Could cholera become an emerging infection in developed countries? New cases have been found in the United States as a result of travel from an endemic area, where cases are found at a constantly low level in the population. These cases have been found to be associated with importing and eating contaminated food, and with aging or improperly maintained water purification and sewage treatment facilities. The overuse of antibiotics has created cholera (and other) bacteria that are resistant to this kind of treatment.

Because *Vibrio* bacilli can enter a noncultivatable state but still remain infectious, this means that water supplies that may test negative for the presence of these bacteria may, in fact, be unsafe. When a new strain of cholera bacillus appeared in Bengal recently, it was shown that this strain (*Vibrio cholerae* O139) became dormant within a week, even at cool temperatures. New strains of cholera bacilli may be considered emerging pathogens. Future human activities such as those that promote global warming will also contribute to the possible emergence of cholera infections in areas where it has not usually been found.

THE POSSIBILITIES FOR NEW TREATMENT METHODS
Modern scientists have a renewed respect for traditional medicines used in different cultures, and this may provide opportunities for finding new medications for treatment and prevention of diseases. In Japan and China, diarrheal diseases have been controlled by herbal medicine preparations called Kampe formulations for centuries. Recently, the chemicals within these herbal medicines have been isolated and characterized. These medicines have been shown to inhibit all cholera

toxin activities. It is suggested that the most active component of these ancient medications could be added to the latest formulation for oral replacement therapy in order to help control the severe diarrhea of cholera.

Another novel approach uses more modern recombinant DNA technologies. The gene for determining cholera toxin has been cut out and spliced into the genes of potatoes. Mice that were fed these genetically altered potatoes became immune to cholera infection. The ability to incorporate these genes in plants (such as rice) may enable doctors to distribute vaccinations simply by telling their patients which foods to eat. This is another direction scientific research may take in order to improve the treatment and prevention of cholera and other infectious diseases in the future.

CHOLERA ON GENE CHIPS

Once scientists had mapped out the entire cholera genome, they could utilize the new technology of **gene chips**. To create a gene chip, scientists place tiny dots of DNA segments onto a glass plate in a regular pattern. This is referred to as a microarray. Next, genes from any source can be labeled (this is referred to as a probe and often contains a fluorescent or radioactive marker) and then allowed to hybridize on the microarray. Genes that hybridize to the probe will display the label. In this way, scientists can identify genes that match those of the probe. This technique has been used to compare different strains of cholera bacilli such as those found in endemic areas and those found during epidemics. It does appear that cholera strains that can incorporate a cluster of genes called a TCP pathogenicity island and the filamentous phage CTΦ (and perhaps a few other antigenic proteins) can become pathogenic to humans. The TCP pathogenicity island is a group of genes that encode for TCP pili, a colonization factor and receptor for CTXΦ (the filamentous cholera toxin phage), and toxR, an essential virulence regulation gene. These results need further testing and verification, but the methods used will enable very precise definition of pathogenicity in these microorganisms at the genetic level.

WARS

Like poverty, war is a breeding ground for many infectious diseases, and cholera is no exception. In August 2007, cholera broke out in Kirkuk, in northern Iraq. It spread to 18 provinces. Overall, there were about 30,000 Iraqis who developed cholera-like symptoms.

In areas of Iraq where water is unclean and raw sewage is near the water supply, cholera abounds. These areas also harbor the insurgents in this war. Because insurgents were using chlorine in bombing attacks, the chemical was restricted in many insurgent areas; this lack of chlorine meant that the water supply in these areas went untreated, leaving people vulnerable to cholera outbreaks.[1]

GLOBAL CLIMATE CHANGE

It can be difficult to connect global climate change to the spread of a disease. However, since the 1970s, human infectious diseases have been increasing worldwide. These diseases include dengue fever, malaria, West Nile virus, and Lyme disease. WHO estimates that 150,000 lives are lost each year as a result of infectious diseases as well as noninfectious problems such as heat stroke and asthma, as a result of climate change.

The connection between climate change and cholera outbreaks is much clearer than that for other infectious diseases. As temperatures of the oceans increase, so do algal blooms, the diet of copepods. Using data obtained through remote-sensing and satellite imagery, information about sea levels, chlorophyll content of seas, and sea temperatures, scientists can predict the incidence of cholera four months in advance of potential outbreaks. This predictor model has worked well in Bangladesh and Peru in recent years.

Applying similar models, scientists may one day be able to predict the incidence of other infectious diseases in order to act to forestall or prevent outbreaks. In this way, the study of cholera may help scientists understand and prevent other infectious diseases.

CHOLERA AND BIOTERRORISM

The Federation of American Scientists recently listed some microorganisms that may be used for biological warfare. In addition to diseases such as anthrax, plague, and the Ebola virus, cholera is on this list as well. Why might cholera be considered as an agent for biological warfare? The goals of bioterrorists are to disrupt society and to promote unrest. Killing is not necessarily, and not always, a primary goal in warfare. Creating large numbers of sick, disabled persons would sorely tax any nation's resources. Cholera could be used to contaminate unguarded water supplies. Massive numbers of cases would tax medical resources, possibly making the society more vulnerable to other types of attacks. Present vaccines are only about 50 percent effective, and the immunity they provide lasts less than a year, often only about six months. Antibiotics have a limited effect. In reality, water supplies in developed countries would most likely eliminate contaminating cholera microorganisms before they could harm anyone. Developed countries practice good sanitation and treat water supplies with chlorine or other halides regularly. Cholera bacilli are susceptible to these treatments. Further, water supplies are regularly monitored for fecal contamination. Public sewage areas are also treated and monitored for fecal contamination. However, should the water treatment somehow fail, cholera might survive and could make thousands very sick. Obviously, terrorists are aware of this, too.

MEETING THESE CHALLENGES

Cholera bacilli are part of the estimated 2 to 3 percent of all microorganisms on Earth that are known to cause disease.

Free-living *Vibrios* produce no toxin. However, when in contact with human waste, the toxin is produced. There is no known function for the cholera toxin in nature. Ordinarily, these bacteria serve to recycle organic matter in waters. Toxin formation is not needed for its survival in this environment. The ability of this microorganism to form a toxin changes human behaviors. Both microbes and humans will, out of necessity, continue to share this planet. Each must adapt to the other for survival. The challenges of global warming, bioterrorism, and war must be met with international cooperation if cholera is to be controlled. Infectious microorganisms do not recognize national borders. Understanding a specific infectious disease such as cholera continues to present new ways to intervene in its growth cycle. However, human activities and political realities also pose new challenges for the future.

Notes

Chapter 1

1. Steven Johnson, *The Ghost Map: The Story of London's Most Terrifying Epidemic—and How It Changed Science, Cities, and the Modern World* (New York: Riverhead Books, 2006).

Chapter 2

1. S. Faruque, D. Sack, B. Sack, R. Colwell, Y. Takeda, and B. Nair, "Emergence and evolution of *Vibrio cholerae* O139," *Proceedings of the National Academy of Sciences of the United States of America* 100 (2003): 1304–1309.
2. A. Guidolin and P.A. Manning, "Genetics of *Vibrio Cholerae* and Its Bacteriophages," *Microbiological Reviews* 51, 2 (1987): 285–98.
3. M.K. Waldor and D. I. Friedman, "Phage Regulatory Circuits and Virulence Gene Expression," *Current Opinion in Microbiology* 8, 4 (2005): 459–465.
4. E. Jouravleva, G. McDonald, C. Garon, M. Boesman-Finkelstein, and R. Finkelstein, "Characterization and possible functions of a new filamentous bacteriophage from *Vibrio cholerae* O139," *Microbiology* 144 (1998): 315–324.
5. J.G. Lawrence, "Horizontal and Vertical Gene Transfer: The Life History of Pathogens," *Contributions to Microbiology* 12 (2005): 255–271.

Chapter 3

1. R. Colwell, "From Cholera to Complexity to Society: A Journey to New Dimensions" (keynote speech, National Science Foundation, June 29, 2002), http://www.nsf.gov/news/speeches/colwell/rc020629rutgers.htm, (accessed June 12, 2008).
2. G. Fleming, M. Merwe, and G. McFerren, "Fuzzy Expert Systems and GIS for Cholera Health Risk Prediction in Southern Africa," *Environmental Modelling and Software* 22, 4 (2007): 442–448.
3. M. Ali, M. Emch, J.P. Donnay, M. Yunus, and R.B. Sack, "Identifying Environmental Risk Factors for Endemic Cholera: a Raster GIS Approach," *Health and Place* 8, 3 (2002): 201–210.
4. L. Beck, U. Kitron, and M. Bobo, "Remote sensing, GIS, and spatial statistics: powerful tools for landscape epidemiology," in *Environmental Change, Climate, and Health: Issues and Research Methods*, eds. P. Martens, W.J. Meine, and A. J. McMichael. (Cambridge, UK: Cambridge University Press, 2002), 226–252.
5. Alan Dove, "News Feature: Eye in the Sky." *Nature Medicine* 10, 11 (2004): 1151.
6. S. Paz and M. Broza, "Wind Direction and Its Linkage with *Vibrio Cholerae* Dissemination," *Environmental Health Perspectives* 115, 2 (2007): 195–200.

Chapter 4

1. S. Levy, "Cholera's Life Aquatic," *Bioscience—Washington* 55, 9 (2005): 728–733.
2. A. Huq, E.B. Small, P.A. West, M.I. Huq, R. Rahman, and R.R. Colwell, "Ecological Relationships between *Vibrio Cholerae* and Planktonic Crustacean Copepods," *Applied and Environmental Microbiology* 45, 1 (1983): 275–283.
3. M. Islam, S. Mahmuda, M. Morshed, H. Bakht, M. Khan, R. Sack, and D. Sack, "Role of cyanobacteria in the persistence of *Vibrio cholerae* O139 in saline microcosms," *Canadian Journal of Microbiology* 50 (2004): 127–131.
4. D.B. Araujo, S.C.S. Martins, L.M.B. de Albuquerque, and E. Hofer, "Influence of the Copepod *Mesocyclops Longisetus* (Crustacea: Cyclopidae) on the Survival of *Vibrio Cholerae* O1 in Fresh Water," *Cadernos De Sau de Publica* 12, 4: (1996) 551–554.
5. M. Baker, "What cholera can teach us about climate change," *Stanford Medicine Magazine* Spring 2007, http://stanmed.stanford.edu/2007spring/cholera.html, (accessed May 12, 2008).
6. R.E. Vance, J. Zhu, and J.J. Mekalanos, "A Constitutively Active Variant of the Quorum-Sensing Regulator LuxO Affects Protease Production and Biofilm

Formation in *Vibrio Cholerae,*" *Infection and Immunity* 71 (2003): 2571–2576.

7. D.C. Griffith, L. A. Kelly-Hope, and M. A. Miller, "Review of Reported Cholera Outbreaks Worldwide, 1995–2005," *American Journal of Tropical Medicine and Hygiene* 75, 5 (2006): 973–977.

8. R. Tauxe, "Cholera," in *Bacterial Infections in Humans: Epidemiology and Control.* eds. A. Evans and P. Brockman (New York: Plenum, 1998).

9. Robert F. Stock, *Cholera in Africa: Diffusion of the Disease 1970–1975, with Particular Emphasis on West Africa,* African environment : Special report, 3. (London: International African Institute, 1976).

Chapter 5

1. M.A. Gordon, A.L. Walsh, S.R. Rogerson, K.C. Magomero, C.E. Machili, J.E. Corkill, and C.A. Hart, "Three Cases of Bacteremia Caused by *Vibrio Cholerae* O1 in Blantyre, Malawi," *Emerging Infectious Diseases* 7, 6 (2001).

2. Y. Sakaue, Y. Yoshida, T. Iida, K. Park, and T. Honda, "An imported cholera case infected with both O139 synonym Bengal and O1 *Vibrio cholerae* in Japan," *European Journal of Epidemiology* 11, (1995): 713–714

3. N.A. Bhuiyan, F. Qadri, A.S.G. Faruque, M.A. Malek, M.A. Salam, F. Nato, J.M. Fournier, S. Chanteau, D.A. Sack, and G.B. Nair, "Use of Dipsticks for Rapid Diagnosis of Cholera Caused by *Vibrio Cholerae* O1 and O139 from Rectal Swabs," *Journal of Clinical Microbiology* 41, (2003): 3939–3941.

Chapter 6

1. S.R. Blanke, "Portals and Pathways: Principles of Bacterial Toxin Entry into Host Cells," *Microbe—American Society of Microbiology* 1, 1 (2006): 26–32.

2. W.I. Lencer, and B. Tsai, "The Intracellular Voyage of Cholera Toxin: Going Retro," *Trends in Biochemical Sciences—Monthly Edition* 28, 12 (2003): 639–645.

Chapter 7

1. D. Raskin, J. Bina, and J. Mekalanos, "Genomic and Genetic Analysis of *Vibrio Cholerae,*" *ASM News—American Society for Microbiology* 70 (2004): 57–62.

2. M. Dziejman, E. Balon, D. Boyd, C. M. Fraser, J.F. Heidelberg, and J.J. Mekalanos, "Comparative Genomic Analysis of *Vibrio Cholerae*: Genes That Correlate with Cholera Endemic and Pandemic Disease," *Proceedings—National Academy of Sciences USA* 99 (2002): 1556–1561.

3. J. Bina, J. Zhu, M. Dziejman, S. Faruque, S. Calderwood, and J. Mekalanos, "ToxR Regulon of *Vibrio Cholerae* and Its Expression in Vibrios Shed by Cholera Patients," *Proceedings—National Academy of Sciences USA,* 100 (2003): 2801–2806.

4. D.S. Merrell, S.M. Butler, F. Qadri, N.A. Dolganov, A. Alam, M.B. Cohen, S.B. Calderwood, G.K. Schoolnik, and A. Camilli, "Letters to Nature—Host-Induced Epidemic Spread of the Cholera Bacterium," *Nature* 417, 6889 (2002): 642.

5. M. Camara, A. Hardman, P. Williams, and D. Milton, "Quorum Sensing in *Vibrio Cholerae,*" *Nature Genetics* 32 (2002): 217–218.

6. C.M. Walters, W. Lu, J.D. Rabinowitz, and B.L. Bassler, "Quorum Sensing Controls Biofilm Formation in *Vibrio Cholerae* Through Modulation of Cyclic Di-GMP Levels and Repression of VpsT," *Journal of Bacteriology* 190, 7 (2008): 2527–2536.

Chapter 8

1. R.L. Guerrant, "Editorials: Cholera—Still Teaching Hard Lessons," *The New England Journal of Medicine* 355, 23 (2006): 2500.

2. D. Saha, "Single-Dose Azithromycin for the Treatment of Cholera in Adults," *The New England Journal of Medicine,* 355, 23 (2006): 2452.

Notes

Chapter 9

1. R.R. Colwell, et al, "Reduction of Cholera in Bangladeshi Villages by Simple Filtration," *Proceedings of the National Academy of Sciences of the United States of America*, 100, 3 (2003): 1051–1055.
2. M.P. Girard, D. Steele, C.L. Chaignat, and M.P. Kieny, "A Review of Vaccine Research and Development: Human Enteric Infections," *Vaccine*, 24, 15 (2006): 2732–2750.
3. David Bello, "Scientists dish up rice vaccine to fight cholera," *Scientific Amercan*, June 11, 2007, http://www.sciam.com/article.cfm?id=scientists-dish-up-rice-vaccine-to-fight-cholera, (accessed May 12, 2008).
4. T. Nochi, H. Takagi, Y. Yuki, L. Yang, T. Masumura, M. Mejima, U. Nakanishi, A. Matsumura, A. Uozumi, and T. Hiroi, "Rice-Based Mucosal Vaccine As a Global Strategy for Cold-Chain- and Needle-Free Vaccination," *Proceedings—National Academy of Sciences USA* 104, 26 (2007): 10986–10991.

Chapter 10

1. Mark Drapeau, "A Microscopic Insurgent." *New York Times,* December 4, 2007, http://www.nytimes.com/2007/12/04/opinion/04drapeau.html?scp=1&sq=microscopic%20insurgent&st=cse, (accessed May 12, 2008).

acidosis—Increase of acidity in blood serum.

adenyl cyclase—An enzyme that forms cyclic AMP from ATP.

aerobic—In the presence of oxygen.

agar—A semisolid polymer made from seaweed that is used to hold nutrients that bacteria require for growth.

alimentary canal—The connection from mouth to anus.

alpha (α) helix—A spiral structure that gives form to some proteins.

anaerobic—In the absence of oxygen.

annotated sequence—A sequence of DNA for which the protein product and/or function is known.

antibiotic—Drug that kills bacteria.

antibody—Proteins formed in the blood serum in response to antigens.

antigen—A substance that induces the formation of antibodies.

asymptomatic—The state of an infected patient in which there are no symptoms or evidence of that infection.

attenuate—To weaken.

autoinducers—Quorum-sensing chemicals produced by bacteria.

bacteremia—When bacteria are present in the bloodstream.

bacteriophage—A bacterial virus.

bile salt—A chemical formed by the gallbladder to help digest fats by emulsifying them.

biofilm—Mixtures of microorganisms growing in a natural state.

biotype—Strains of bacteria that are very similar and may have originated from the same strain, yet have different identifying characteristics.

biovar—A variety of a species with shared biological properties.

carrier—An infected individual who can transmit that infection to another individual; often asymptomatic.

cell density—The quantity of cells per unit of volume.

chemotaxis—Movement toward specific chemicals.

Glossary

cholera cot—A special cot with an opening that allows fluid lost in the form of diarrhea to be collected.

clone—A genetically identical organism.

colony—A group of cells that are visible to the naked eye, formed by a single microbe that has divided repeatedly.

commensalisms—A form of parasitism in which both the host and the parasite benefit.

conjugation—A method of bacterial recombination in which DNA is transferred from one strain to another by cell-to-cell contact.

conjugative plasmids—Genetic elements that can be transferred between cells by conjugation.

contagion theory—The belief that diseases are spread directly from person to person.

copepod—A type of invertebrate found as part of zooplankton.

counterstain—A stain used to contrast another in procedures when more than one stain is used.

communication of disease—How a disease is spread in a population.

cyclic AMP—A chemical involved in controlling cell metabolism.

defecate—To eliminate solid waste.

diarrhea—Loose or watery bowel movements.

electrolytes—Substances dissolved in solutions that are positively or negatively charged; for example, ions in water.

emerging infectious disease—A newly recognized infectious disease, often a result of human activity.

endemic—Describes a disease that is found in a particular place all year long.

endopeptidase—An enzyme that breaks peptide bonds in the interior of a protein.

endotoxin—The lipopolysaccharide of Gram negative bacteria that is a factor in their ability to cause disease.

epidemic—An increase in the number of disease cases above the normally expected number of cases.

epidemiology—The study of disease transmission, incidence, and control.

epithelium—The outermost layer of the skin or related tissues.

eukaryote—A cell that contains a true nucleus (membranes surrounding the genetic material).

facultative—Ability to live under different conditions.

feces—Solid waste.

filamentous virus—A virus with a linear shape.

fluid replacement therapy—Treatment with water and electrolytes to replace those that are lost, often as a result of infection.

fungi (singular: **fungus**)—Eukaryotic saprophytic kingdom of organisms; also called molds.

ganglioside—A unique type of lipid associated with cell membrane structure; glycolipids with a complex carbohydrate group.

gene chips—Genetic material for specific traits placed on slides that can be identified by hybridization.

gene expression—The conversion of the information encoded in a gene first into messenger RNA and then to a protein.

germ theory of disease—The theory that infectious diseases are caused by specific microorganisms.

glycolipid—A lipid containing a carbohydrate group.

Gram stain reaction—A procedure that visualizes bacteria and determines if they retain crystal violet dye (Gram positive) or do not (Gram negative).

GTP—Guanosine triphosphate; a nucleotide.

hemagglutination—Clumping of red blood cells.

hemolysis—Bursting of red blood cells.

holotoxin—A toxin, including its protein and all other chemical factors.

hypertonic—Solution higher in electrolytes than a standard.

hypoglycemia—Low levels of glucose in the blood.

hypothesis—An educated guess that is testable; part of the scientific method of problem solving.

hypotonic—Solution lower in electrolytes when compared to a standard.

hypovolemia—Low fluid volume of the blood.

Glossary

incidence—The number of new cases of a disease that arise over a specific period of time.

incubation period—The time after infection and before disease symptoms first appear.

initiator codon—The set of three bases in messenger RNA that is the first set to be translated into a polypeptide during protein synthesis.

integron island—Genes that specify a system of proteins that allows the capture of foreign genes.

intravenous (IV)—Injection into a vein.

kilobase—One thousand nucleic acid bases.

landscape epidemiology—The study of patterns of disease transmission related to the geographic landscape.

lipid A—A lipid in the outer membranes of Gram negative bacteria.

LPS (lipopolysaccharide)—Lipids in the outer membranes of Gram negative bacteria.

lumen—The interior of a hollow body organ.

lysogeny—Incorporation of a bacterial genome into that of its bacterial host without lysing (bursting) that host.

maintenance therapy—Treatment to reduce immediate symptoms of a disease and to stabilize a patient.

medium (plural: **media**)—Term to indicate the substance used for growth of microorganisms in culture.

miasma—The invisible emanation of toxins or harmful materials thought to carry disease.

microorganism—Life form requiring a microscope to see.

monoclonal antibodies—Homogeneous (identical) antibodies that react against a single antigen.

monovalent vaccine—An antigen preparation that induces the formation of antibodies against a single strain of bacteria.

morbidity—The number of dead plus the number of infected, but living, individuals.

mortality—The number of deaths from an infectious disease.

motile—Able to move, often because a microbe has flagella.

mucin—Protein in mucous secretions, many of which contain polysaccharides.

mutagen—A chemical that can damage DNA and cause mutants to be formed.

NAD (nicotinamide adenine dinucleotide)—A common enzyme cofactor that carries hydrogen in cells; it is key to energy generation by cells.

normal flora—Microorganisms normally found in healthy individuals.

oligomeric—Molecules such as proteins made up of several subunits.

oliguria—Urinating less than usual.

ORF (open reading frame)—A DNA sequence between the initiator codon and the terminator codon.

pandemic—A global epidemic.

pathogen—A microbe that can cause disease.

pathogenic—The ability of a microorganism to cause disease.

pathogenicity island—A cluster of genes that determine characteristics that make a microorganism able to cause disease.

phage typing—The identification of strains of bacteria by finding the bacteriophages to which they are susceptible.

phagocytic cells—Cells capable of ingesting other cells and other materials.

phosphodiesterase—An enzyme that attacks cyclic AMP (cAMP), converting it to AMP.

pili (singular: **pillus**)—Hairlike projections from some bacteria.

plasmid—A genetic element outside the chromosome in the cytoplasm of cells.

polyvalent vaccine—An antigen preparation that induces the formation of antibodies against more than one strain of a microorganism.

porin—A protein in the outer membranes of Gram negative bacteria that permits transport of materials across that membrane.

prokaryote—A cell without a true nucleus.

prophylactic—Preventative.

pure culture—A population of microorganisms arising from a single cell; a clone.

Glossary

quorum sensing—The ability of cells to communicate with other cells through chemicals they produce.

recombinant DNA—DNA formed in laboratories using DNA from more than one species.

regulatory proteins—Proteins that function to change the production or activity of other proteins, particularly enzymes.

sanitation—Promoting hygiene by reducing the numbers of microorganisms in a location.

self-limiting infection—An infection that a person can control naturally with his or her immune system.

serogroup—A group of distinct microorganisms that can react with one antibody preparation.

serotype—Strains of an organism that are distinguished by different immunological reactions.

skin turgor—The tightness of the skin.

slide agglutination—The clumping reaction of antigens and antibodies on a glass slide.

spores—The resting state of some bacteria. Under suitable conditions they germinate to produce bacteria. Spore-forming bacteria are a health hazard because they can survive pasteurization and sterilization.

stool specimen—Sample of fecal waste.

streak plate method—Using sterilized wire (inoculating needles) to place microbes on agar plates in order to isolate individual clones (colonies).

synergistic—Cooperation such that combined effects are greater than that of either participant.

temperate virus—A virus that induces lysogeny after infecting a host.

terminator codon—The "stop" signal in the DNA code that signals the end of a transcription.

tissue culture—Growth of animal or plant cells, in tubes or plates, outside of the tissues they came from.

toxoid—Modified toxin that remains antigenic but that is no longer toxic.

transduction—Method for gene recombination in microorganisms in which a virus carries DNA between cells.

transmission—The spread of a disease.

ubiquitin—A natural chemical used by cells to tap proteins for recognition, particularly by degradation enzymes.

vaccine—An antigenic preparation used to prevent infection by inducing formation of protective antibodies.

villi (singular: **villus**)—A finger-like projection of cells lining the intestinal tract.

virulent—The ability of a pathogenic microorganism to cause severe disease.

Bibliography

Ali, M., M. Emch, J. P. Donnay, M. Yunus, and R. B. Sack. "Identifying Environmental Risk Factors for Endemic Cholera: a Raster GIS Approach." *Health and Place* 8, 3 (2002): 201–210.

Araujo, D.B., S.C.S. Martins, L.M.B. de Albuquerque, and E. Hofer. "Influence of the Copepod Mesocyclops Longisetus (Crustacea: Cyclopidae) on the Survival of Vibrio Cholerae O1 in Fresh Water." *Cadernos De Sau de Publica* 12, 4 (1996): 551–554.

Baker, M. "What cholera can teach us about climate change." *Stanford Medicine Magazine* (Spring 2007). Available online. URL: http://stanmed.stanford.edu/2007spring/cholera.html. Accessed May 12, 2008.

Bello, David. "Scientists dish up rice vaccine to fight cholera." *Scientific Amercan* (June 11, 2007). Available online. URL: http://www.sciam.com/article.cfm?id=scientists-dish-up-rice-vaccine-to-fight-cholera. Accessed May 12, 2008.

Bhuiyan, N.A., F. Qadri, A.S.G. Faruque, M.A. Malek, M.A. Salam, F. Nato, J.M. Fournier, S. Chanteau, D.A. Sack, and G.B. Nair. "Use of Dipsticks for Rapid Diagnosis of Cholera Caused by Vibrio Cholerae O1 and O139 from Rectal Swabs." *Journal of Clinical Microbiology* 41 (2003): 3939–3941.

Bina, J., J. Zhu, M. Dziejman, S. Faruque, S. Calderwood, and J. Mekalanos. "ToxR Regulon of Vibrio Cholerae and Its Expression in Vibrios Shed by Cholera Patients." *Proceedings—National Academy of Sciences USA* 100 (2003): 2801–2806.

Blanke, Steven R. "Portals and Pathways: Principles of Bacterial Toxin Entry into Host Cells." *Microbe—American Society of Microbiology* 1, 1 (2006): 26–32.

Camara, M., A. Hardman, P. Williams, and D. Milton. "Quorum Sensing in Vibrio Cholerae." *Nature Genetics* 32 (2002): 217–218.

Colwell R.R., et al. "Reduction of Cholera in Bangladeshi Villages by Simple Filtration." *Proceedings of the National Academy of Sciences of the United States of America* 100, 3 (2003): 1051–1055.

Colwell, R., "From Cholera to Complexity to Society: A Journey to New Dimensions." Keynote Speech: National Science Foundation, June 29, 2002. Available online. URL: http://www.nsf.gov/news/speeches/colwell/rc020629rutgers.htm. Accessed June 12, 2008.

Dove, Alan. "News Feature: Eye in the Sky." *Nature Medicine* 10, 11 (2004): 1151.

Drapeau, Mark. "A Microscopic Insurgent." *New York Times,* December 4, 2007. Available online. URL: http://www.nytimes.com/2007/12/04/opinion/04drapeau.html?scp=1&sq=microscopic%20insurgent&st=cse. Accessed May 12, 2008.

Dziejman, M., E. Balon, D. Boyd, C.M. Fraser, J.F. Heidelberg, and J.J. Mekalanos. "Comparative Genomic Analysis of Vibrio Cholerae: Genes That Correlate with Cholera Endemic and Pandemic Disease." *Proceedings—National Academy of Sciences USA* 99 (2002): 1556–1561.

Faruque, S.M., D.A. Sack, R.B. Sack, R.R. Colwell, Y. Takeda, and G.B. Nair. "Emergence and Evolution of Vibrio Cholerae O139." *Proceedings— National Academy of Sciences USA* 100 (2003): 1304–1309.

Finkelstein, Richard A. "Cholera, Vibrio cholerae O1 and O139, and Other Pathogenic Vibrios." in *Medical Microbiology.* Patrick R Murray, ed. St. Louis: Mosby, 2002. Available online. URL: http://gsbs.utmb.edu/microbook/ch024.htm. Accessed May 12, 2008.

Fleming, G., M. Merwe, and G. McFerren. "Fuzzy Expert Systems and GIS for Cholera Health Risk Prediction in Southern Africa." *Environmental Modelling and Software* 22, 4 (2007): 442–448.

Girard M.P., D. Steele, C.L. Chaignat, and M.P. Kieny. "A Review of Vaccine Research and Development: Human Enteric Infections." *Vaccine* 24, 15 (2006): 2732–2750.

Griffith, D.C., L.A. Kelly-Hope, and M.A. Miller. "Review of Reported Cholera Outbreaks Worldwide, 1995–2005." *American Journal of TropicalMedicine and Hygiene* 75, 5 (2006): 973–977.

Guerrant, R.L. "Cholera—Still Teaching Hard Lessons." *New England Journal of Medicine* 354, 23 (2006): 2500–2502.

Guidolin A., and P.A. Manning. "Genetics of *Vibrio Cholerae* and Its Bacteriophages." *Microbiological Reviews,* 51, 2 (1987): 285–298.

Huq A., E.B. Small, P.A. West, M.I. Huq, R. Rahman, and R.R. Colwell. "Ecological Relationships between *Vibrio Cholerae* and Planktonic Crustacean Copepods." *Applied and Environmental Microbiology* 45, 1 (1983): 275–283.

Islam, M.S., S. Mahmuda, M.G. Morshed, H.B.M. Bakht, M.N.H. Khan, R.B. Sack, and D.A. Sack. "Role of Cyanobacteria in the Persistence of Vibrio Cholerae O139 in Saline Microcosms." *Canadian Journal of Microbiology* 50 (2004): 127–131.

Bibliography

Johnson, Steven. *The Ghost Map: The Story of London's Most Terrifying Epidemic—and How It Changed Science, Cities, and the Modern World.* New York: Riverhead Books, 2006.

Jouravleva E.A., G.A. McDonald, C.F. Garon, M. Boesman-Finkelstein, and R.A. Finkelstein. "Characterization and Possible Functions of a New Filamentous Bacteriophage from Vibrio Cholerae O139." *Microbiology* (Reading, England) 144 (1998): 315–324.

Lawrence, J.G. "Horizontal and Vertical Gene Transfer: The Life History of Pathogens." *Contributions to Microbiology* 12 (2005): 255–271.

Lencer, W.I., and B. Tsai. "The Intracellular Voyage of Cholera Toxin: Going Retro." *Trends in BiochemicalSciences—Monthly Edition* 28, 12 (2003): 639–645.

Levy, S. "Cholera's Life Aquatic." *Bioscience—Washington* 55, 9 (2005): 728–733.

Martens, Willem Jozef Meine, and A.J. McMichael. *Environmental Change, Climate, and Health: Issues and Research Methods.* Cambridge, UK: Cambridge University Press, 2002.

Merrell, D.S., S.M. Butler, F. Qadri, N.A. Dolganov, A. Alam, M.B. Cohen, S.B. Calderwood, G.K. Schoolnik, and A. Camilli. "Letters to Nature—Host-Induced Epidemic Spread of the Cholera Bacterium." *Nature* 417, 6889 (2002): 642.

Nochi, T., H. Takagi, Y. Yuki, L. Yang, T. Masumura, M. Mejima, U. Nakanishi, A. Matsumura, A. Uozumi, and T. Hiroi. "Rice-Based Mucosal Vaccine As a Global Strategy for Cold-Chain-and Needle-Free Vaccination." *Proceedings—National Academy of Sciences USA* 104, 26 (2007): 10986–10991.

Paz, S., and M. Broza. "Wind Direction and Its Linkage with Vibrio Cholerae Dissemination." *Environmental Health Perspectives* 115, 2 (2007): 195–200.

Raskin, D., J. Bina, and J. Mekalanos. "Genomic and Genetic Analysis of Vibrio Cholerae." *ASM News—American Society for Microbiology* 70 (2004): 57–62.

Saha, D. "Single-Dose Azithromycin for the Treatment of Cholera in Adults." *New England Journal of Medicine* 355, 23 (2006): 2452.

Sakaue, Y., H. Yoshida, T. Iida, K.S. Park, and T. Honda. "An Imported Cholera Case Infected with Both O139 Synonym Bengal and O1 Vibrio Cholerae in Japan." *European Journal of Epidemiology* 11, 6 (1995): 713–714.

Schild, S., A. Bishop, and A. Camilli. "Ins and outs of *Vibrio cholerae*." *Microbe* 3 (2008): 131–136. Available online. URL: http://www.asm.org/microbe/index.asp?bid=56849. Accessed May 12, 2008.

Vance, R.E., J. Zhu, and J.J. Mekalanos. "A Constitutively Active Variant of the Quorum-Sensing Regulator LuxO Affects Protease Production and Biofilm Formation in Vibrio Cholerae." *Infection and Immunity* 71 (2003): 2571–2576.

Waldor, M.K., and D.I. Friedman. "Phage Regulatory Circuits and Virulence Gene Expression." *Current Opinion in Microbiology* 8, 4 (2005): 459–465.

Waters, Christopher M., Wenyun Lu, Joshua D. Rabinowitz, and Bonnie L. Bassler. "Quorum Sensing Controls Biofilm Formation in Vibrio Cholerae Through Modulation of Cyclic Di-GMP Levels and Repression of VpsT." *Journal of Bacteriology* 190, 7 (2008): 2527.

Further Resources

Books and Articles

Alcamo, E. *Fundamentals of Microbiology*. 6th ed. Boston: Jones and Bartlett, 2001.

Bannister, B., N. Begg, and S. Gillespie. *Infectious Disease*. Cambridge: Blackwell Science, 1996.

Barua, D., and W. Greenough, editors. *Cholera*. New York: Plenum Medical Book Company, 1992.

Belkin, Shimshon, and Rita R. Colwell. *Oceans and Health: Pathogens in the Marine Environment*. New York: Springer Science+Business Media, 2006.

Colwell, R., and J. Grimes, editors. *Nonculturable Microorganisms in the Environment*. Washington, D.C.: ASM Press, 2000.

Evans, A., and P. Brockman, editors. *Cholera*. New York: Plenum, 1998.

Ewald, P. *Evolution of Infectious Disease*. New York. Oxford University Press, 1993.

Ewald, Paul W. *Plague Time: The New Germ Theory of Diease*. New York: Anchor Books, 2002.

Farthing, M. and G. Keusch, editors. *Enteric Infections, Mechanisms, Manifestations and Management*. New York: Raven Press, 1989.

Feigin, Ralph D. *Textbook of Pediatric Infectious Diseases*. Philadelphia: Saunders, 2004.

Gest, H. *The World of Microbes*. San Francisco: Benjamin Cummings, 1988.

Goering, Richard V., and Cedric A. Mims. *Mims' Medical Microbiology*. Philadelphia: Mosby Elsevier, 2008.

Goodwin, C., editor. *Cholera and Other Vibrios*. Melbourne, Australia: Blackwell, 1984.

Johnson, Steven. *The Ghost Map: The Story of London's Deadliest Epidemic, and How It Changed the Way We Think About Disease, Cities, Science, and the Modern World*. New York: Riverhead, 2006.

Mims, C., A. Nash, and J. Stephen. *The Pathogenesis of Infectious Disease*. San Diego: Academic Press, 2001.

Murray, P., K. Rosenthal, G. Kobayashi, and M. Pfaller. *Medical Microbiology*. St. Louis: Mosby, 1997.

Salyers, A. and D. Whitt, *Microbiology, Disease, Diversity and the Environment*. Bethesda, Md.: Fitzgerald Science Press, 2001.

Web Sites

American Museum of Natural History, Water Exhibit
http://www.amnh.org/exhibitions/water

Microbiology Bytes: Bacteriophages
http://www.microbiologybytes.com/virology/Phages.html

USGenNet: Sickness and Death in the Old South
http://www.tngenweb.org/darkside/cholera.html

World Health Organization (WHO)
http://www.who.int/topics/cholera/en

Index

Ab. *See* antibody
AB toxin, 71–73, 76
acidosis, 60
adenosine diphosphate-
    ribosylation factor 6
    (ARF6), 74
adenosine triphosphate
    (ATP). *See* ATP
adenyl cyclase, 69, 70
ADP-ribose, 74, 75
aerobic, 23
aeroplankton, 43
Ag. *See* antigen
agar, 18, 19, 22, 23, 65
agent 0129, 97
air, as carrier of disease, 10
algae, 42, 114, 117
alimentary canal, 36
alkaline peptone, 23, 24, 65
allosteric activator, 74
alpha-GTP protein, 75
alpha helix, 71, 77
alpha subunit, 74, 75
amputation, 12
anaerobic, 23
analytical epidemiology, 41
anesthesia, 34–35
annotated sequence, 77
antacids, 55
antibiotic(s), 63, 94–99,
    102, 118, 123. *See also*
    specific antibiotics, e.g.:
    ciprofloxacin
antibiotic resistance, 31–32,
    51, 63, 82, 94–99, 102
antibiotic therapy, 63
antibody (Ab), 25, 27–29,
    66
antigen (Ag), 27
antiserum, 64
antitoxin, 106
anuria, 63
A protein, 75
Archaea, 25–26
ARF6 (adenosine diphos-
    phate-ribosylation fac-
    tor 6), 74
Asiatic cholera, 36

A subunit, 71, 73–75, 108
asymptomatic carrier, 27,
    53
ATP (adenosine triphos-
    phate) and cAMP, 68–70
attenuated vaccine, 103,
    105–107
autoinducers, 85–86
azithromycin, 98

bacillus. *See Vibrio*
    cholerae
bacteremia, 58, 66
bacteria, 16, 25. *See also*
    Vibrio cholerae
bacterial virus, 79–82
bacteriophage, 29–31,
    79–80
Bangladesh, 54, 96, 101–
    103, 108, 117
base sequence, 63–64
Bay of Bengal, 46
Bengal, 115
beta subunit, 74
bicarbonate, 91
bile, for inactivated vaccine,
    105
bile salt, 24
biofilm, 47, 82, 85–88
biological warfare, 118
bioluminescence, 86
bioterrorism, 118
biotype, 27
biovar, 50
blood pressure, 59
blood sample, 63
blood type, 55
blue crab, 111
body weight, of patient,
    93–94
boiling, 23, 101
boron, 85–86
bowel sounds, 59
B protein, 73–75
Broad Street, London,
    37–40
B subunit, 71, 73, 106–110
caffeine, 70

Campylobacterium jejuni,
    83
cancer, 76
carbolic acid, 12
carrier, 123
case control method, 41
case studies, 62–64
CDC (Centers for
    Disease Control and
    Prevention), 62
cell density, 47
cell membrane, 22, 26
cellular antigen, 27
Centers for Disease Control
    and Prevention (CDC),
    62
Central America, 52
chemotaxis, 82–83
Chesapeake Bay, 46
Chicago, Illinois, epidemic
    (1849), 49
childbirth fever, 40–41
China, 115
chloramphenicol, 63
chloride ions, 70
chlorine, 101, 117
chlorpromazine, 99
cholera (term), 8, 48
cholera cot, 94, 95
cholera toxin (CT), 71–76
    DNA sequence for, 64
    function, 74–75
    gene for, 79–82
    and human behavior,
        119
    in human environment,
        112
    inhibition by herbal rem-
        edies, 115–116
    and phage conversion,
        30, 80
    and quorum sensing,
        47, 86
    as reagent, 75–76
    ribosylation of myelin
        basic protein by, 76
    structure, 73–74
    and virulence, 67

cholera toxin A (CTA) subunit. *See* A subunit
cholera toxin B (CTB) subunit. *See* B subunit
cholera vaccine, 107–108
chromosome, 25, 77–79
Chromosome 1
   cholera toxin gene, 81
   DNA replication genes, 79
   growth/viability genes, 78
   MCP genes, 83
   nucleic acid base pairs
   on, 78
   TCP formation genes, 80
   toxR regulatory protein,
   81, 82
Chromosome 2
   known proteins coded
   on, 78
   MCP genes, 83
   nucleic acid base pairs
   on, 78
   possible origins of, 79
ciprofloxacin, 98
classical biotype, 27
cleanliness, 12
clean water, 100
climate change, 42, 114,
   117–118
clone, 17
cloth filtration, 101–103,
   114
coconut milk, 55
cohort method, 41
colony, 16–17, 22–23
Colwell, Rita, 45–46
comma bacilli, 19–21
commensalisms, 45, 46
communication of disease,
   36
Comoros Islands, 97
conjugation, 98
conjugative plasmids, 97–98
Connecticut Department of
   Health, 55
contagion theory, 9, 10, 35
convalescent carriers, 47, 61
cooking, 101

copepod, 43, 45, 46, 101–
   103, 111
counterstain, 21
cramps, 59
Crimean War, 12
Crusades, 65
crystal violet, 21, 22, 26
CT. *See* cholera toxin
CTA (cholera toxin A) subunit. *See* A subunit
CTB (cholera toxin B) subunit. *See* B subunit
CTX phage, 30, 46, 51, 80,
   81, 116
current issues, 112–119
CVD 103 strain, 108
cyclic AMP (cAMP), 67–70,
   75, 76
3',5'-cyclic diguanylic acid
   (c-di-GMP), 86–87
cytochrome oxidase, 23
cytoplasm, 25, 32, 72, 73

death from cholera, 51, 61
dehydration, 59, 61, 63, 93
dehydration therapy, 59
Delisea pulchra, 98
descriptive approach, 41
diagnosis, 64–66
diarrhea
   azithromycin treatment,
   98, 99
   and cAMP, 70
   in case study, 62, 63
   and CT, 30
   as first symptom, 57
   herbal remedies, 115
   and IV-ORT, 93
   Newcastle-upon-Tyne
   cholera outbreak, 33
   reduction of volume, 92
   and vaccine testing, 108
dipstick tests, 66
disulfide bond, 71
DNA
   and bacteriophages, 79–80
   on chromosomes 1 and
   2, 79

of eukaryotic cell, 25
in prokaryote, 25
Serogroup O139, 51
and transmission of
   genetic material, 31
for vaccine, 109
and vibriophage, 30
DNA sequence, 64, 83–85
domain bacteria, 25–26
dormant strains, 115
doxycycline, 94, 97
drinking water, 100–103.
   See also water supply
drying, 23
Dukoral, 108

Ecuador, 56
Egypt, 27
electrolytes, 57, 59, 60, 91
El Niño, 42, 46
El Tor strain
   1961 pandemic, 50
   and antibiotic resistance,
   97
   from Ecuador, 56
   first isolation of, 27
   lytic phages in, 30
   peak season for, 54
   vaccine for, 108–109
emerging infectious disease,
   114–115
Emerging Infectious Diseases
   (CDC journal), 62
endemic area, 115
endemic disease, 49
endocytosis pathways, 73
endopeptidase, 73
endoplasmic reticulum, 73
endotoxin, 26
England, 8–10, 35, 37
enrichment procedure, 65
enterotoxin, 30
epidemic, 42–43, 50–55
epidemiology, 36–43
epithelium, 57, 112
erythromycin, 63
Escherichia coli, 83
essential salts, 57

Index

estuaries, 44
ether, 35
ethyl alcohol, 22
eukaryote, 25, 125
experimental epidemiology, 41
extremophiles, 25
eyes, sunken, 59

feces, 47
Federation of American Scientists, 118
fight-or-flight response, 68
filamentous phage CTX, 30, 80, 81
fimbria, 24, 25, 28
flagellar antigen, 27
flagellum, 20, 24, 27, 28, 70
fluid loss, 57–59, 93, 94
fluid replacement therapy, 89, 90–93
fluorescein, 64
fluorescence, 64, 84
fluorescent genomic DNA, 84
fluoroquinoline, 97
folded skin, 90
food, 48, 101, 115
food contamination, 53
Fracastoro, Girolamo, 14
fresh air, 10
furanones, 98
future issues, 112–119

Gama, Vasco da, 48
gamma subunit, 74
ganglioside, 67
ganglioside receptor sites, 75
gastric acid, 55
gelatin, 17–18, 23
gelatin stab culture, 23
gene(s), 78–82
gene chips, 116–117
gene expression, 47, 84
genetic engineering, 109–110, 116

genome, of *Vibrio cholerae*, 77–88
gentamicin, 63
geographical information system (GIS), 42
germ theory of disease, 13–14
global climate change, 115, 117–118
glucose, 69, 91
glycogen, 68
glycolipid, 67, 125
Golgi apparatus, 72
G protein, 74, 75
Gram, Hans Christian, 22
Gram negative, 21, 22, 26
Gram positive, 22, 26
Gram stain reaction, 21, 22, 26
growth medium. *See* medium
GTP (guanosine triphosphate), 74, 75
GTPase, 75
Guerrat, Richard, 98–99

Haffkine, Waldemar, 105
Hamburg, Germany, 10
hand washing, 41
H antigens, 27
HAP, 86
hapR protein, 85, 87
Harnold, John, 9–10, 35, 36
heat inactivation, 105
herbal medicine, 115–116
herd immunity, 110
Hikojima serotype, 27, 28
history, 8–19, 48–51, 65
holotoxin, 73, 125
horizontal transfer, 31–32, 82, 112
horizontal transmission, 31, 51
Horsleydown, London, England, 35–37
hospital infections, 12
host-parasite relationship, 61–62

human environment, 111
hyperinfectious bacteria, 85
hypertonic solutions, 89
hypoglycemia, 60–61
hypothesis, 36

immune response, 27–29
immune system, 62
immunotoxins, 76
Inaba serotype, 27–29, 109, 111
inactivated vaccine, 105, 106, 108
incidence, 53
incubation period, 57
incubatory carriers, 47
India, 35–36, 48, 54
Indian Ocean, 97
indole, 23
Indonesia, 109
initiator codon, 78
Institute for Genomic Research (TIGR), 77
integron island, 78
international travel, 55–56, 100, 111
intestinal cells, 70
intravenous oral replacement therapy (IV-ORT), 93
intravenous rehydration, 63, 89
iodine, 22
ion transport, 69, 70
Iraq, 117
isolation, of *Vibrio cholerae* specimens, 24–25
IV. *See* intravenous *entries*

Japan, 63–64, 115
JBK 70 strain, 106

Kampe formulations, 115
kidney failure, 60
kilobase, 51
Kirkuk, Iraq, 117

Koch, Robert, 14–21, 103, 105
Koch's Postulates, 15, 19
Kolkata, India, 54

landscape epidemiology, 42
Latin American epidemic (1991), 52–54
Legionella pneumophila, 114–115
life cycle, of Vibrio cholerae, 113
lipid A, 26
lipid bilayer, 22, 26
lipopolysaccharide (LPS), 26, 51, 106
Lister, Joseph, 12–13
live vaccine, 105, 109
London, England, 8–10, 35, 37–40
LPS. See lipopolysaccharide
lumen, 70
luminescent Vibrio bacteria, 86
Lusaha, Zambia, 44
lux O protein, 85
lysine amino acids, 73
lysis cycle, 30
lysogenic conversion, 80
lysogenic phage, 29
lysogeny, 29, 30, 80
lytic infection, 29
lytic phage, 30, 46

magnesium, 75
maintenance therapy, 94
Malaysia, 109
mannosensitive hemagglutinin (MSHA), 82
maps, for disease tracking, 37–40, 43
Maryland, 55
medium, 16
mercury, 108
methyl-accepting chemotaxis protein (MCP) gene, 82–83
miasma, 9, 10, 12, 33, 35

microarray, 116
microbe, 16–19, 61–62
Micronesia, 109
microvilli, 69, 112
misfolded proteins, 72–73
monoclonal antibodies, 126
monovalent vaccine, 106
morbidity, 53
mortality, 53, 56, 61
Morton, William, 35
motile bacteria, 20, 127
MSHA (mannosensitive hemagglutinin), 82
mucin, 70, 127
mucosa cells, 72
mucosal cells, 58
Mugabe, Keren, 8
mutagen, 107
mutation, 29, 97, 107
myelin basic protein, 76

NAD (nicotinamide adenine dinucleotide), 74
Napoleon Bonaparte, 65
Nature (journal), 77
neuraminidase enzyme, 84
Newcastle-upon-Tyne, England, 33
New England Journal of Medicine, 98–99
New York City, 49–50
nicotinamide, 74
nicotinamide adenine dinucleotide (NAD), 74
nicotinic acid, 99
Nightingale, Florence, 10–12, 41
nitrosoguanidine, 107
nontoxic strains, 107
normal flora, 62, 127
nucleic acid sequence, 77
nucleotides, 64
nutrition, 99

O1 antigen, 27–29
O1 serogroup, 27
O139 serotype, 27, 50–51, 63

O antigen, 27
O blood type, 55
ocean, 42, 45–46, 86, 111
ofloxacin, 64
Ogawa serotype, 27–29, 111
oligomeric toxin, 71
oliguria, 60
open reading frame (ORF). See ORF
oral rehydration therapy (ORT), 63, 90–93
oral replacement solution (ORS), 91
oral vaccines, 107
ORF (open reading frame), 78
Orochal, 109
ORS (oral replacement solution), 91
ORT. See oral rehydration therapy
Osaka, Japan, 63–64
oysters, 55

Pan American Health Organization, 51
pandemic, 48–55. See also epidemic
parasite, 46, 61–62
Pasteur, Louis, 14, 105
pathogenesis, 82
pathogenic, 67
pathogenicity island, 51, 127
pathogenic microorganism, 67
PCR (polymerase chain reaction), 83
Peru, 89, 98–99, 108, 117
Petri, R. J., 18
petri dish, 18–19
phage conversion, 30
phage typing, 30–31
phagocytic cells, 62
phagocytosis, 51
phosphodiesterase, 69, 70
PilD gene sequence, 82
pili/pillus, 24, 25, 70, 84, 106

Index

plasma membrane receptor, 71
plasmid, 32, 79
Polk, James K., 65
polymerase chain reaction (PCR), 83
polysaccharide capsule, 51
polysaccharides, 27–29, 86
polyvalent vaccine, 106, 107
population studies, 41
porin, 26
positive oxidase reaction, 23
potassium, 61, 92
poverty, 55
pregnancy, 61
prevention, 100–111, 114
prokaryote, 25–26
prophylactic measures, 102
protein, 26, 27, 68, 71, 85, 91. *See also specific proteins, e.g.:* toxR regulatory protein
pulse rate, 59
pure culture, 16

quarantine, 49–50
quorum sensing, 46–47, 85, 98, 112

reagent, 75–76
recombinant DNA, 107–108, 116. *See also* genetic engineering
rectal temperature, 59
refugee camps, 55, 57, 60
regulation pathways, 79
rehydration therapy, 63, 94
renal failure, 63
repeats-in-toxin (RTX) genes, 84
resistant strains. *See* antibiotic resistance
rice, 92
rice vaccine, 109–110
rice water stool, 58
RTX (repeats-in-toxin) genes, 84

safranin, 21, 22, 26
St. Louis, Missouri, 89
sanitation, 12, 41, 47, 53, 98–99. *See also* water supply
sari cloth, 101–103
satellites, for epidemic tracking, 42–43
seafood, 56
sea surface temperature, 42, 43, 46
sec61, 72–73
self-limiting infection, 61
Semmelweis, Ignaz, 40–41
serogroup, 27
serogroup O139, 27, 50–51, 63
serum, 23
serum potassium, 63
sewage treatment plant, 100, 104
side effects, 95–96, 105
Sinai Peninsula, 27
skin turgor, 59
slide agglutination, 29, 63
Snow, John, 9–10, 33–43, 47
sodium, in ORS, 93
sodium bicarbonate, 91
sodium citrate, 91
sodium deoxycholate, 65
sodium ions, 70
sodium pump, 70
somatic antigen, 27
South America, 52
Southeast Asian tsunami (2004), 46
spontaneous generation, 14
spores, 20
S-shaped flask, 14
stabilization, of patient, 94
starch, 23, 91
stool specimen, 24, 64
streak plate method, 16, 17, 19, 24, 128
street vendors, 101
string test, 65
subunit, 71. *See also* A subunit; B subunit

sucrose, 24, 91
sugar-salt solutions, 92
surgery, 12
Surrey Buildings, 36–37
SXT element, 96
symptoms, 57–66
synergistic vaccine preparation, 106

Tanzania, 96
TCBS. *See* thiosulfate-citrate-bile salt-sucrose
Tchaikovsky, Peter Ilych, 65
TCP (toxin-coregulated pilus), 47, 51, 80, 86, 106, 116
temperate phage, 29, 30, 80, 128
temperate phage CTX, 46. *See also* CTX phage
terminator codon, 78
tetracycline, 57, 94, 97, 102
Texas Star-SR, 107
thiosulfate-citrate-bile salt-sucrose (TCBS), 24, 29, 65
TIGR (Institute for Genomic Research), 77
tissue culture, 24
tourism, 66
toxin. *See* cholera toxin
toxin-coregulated pilus (TCP). *See* TCP
toxoid, 106, 107, 128
toxR regulatory protein, 81, 84
transduction, 80, 128
transmission
of cholera, 20, 40, 44–48
of genetic material, 31
transport channel system, 76
treatments, for cholera, 89–99, 115–116
Truscott's Court, 36–37
tsunami (Southeast Asia, 2004), 46
tuberculosis, 16, 19

ubiquitin, 73

vaccine, 82, 102–103, 105–
   110, 118. *See also specific
   vaccines*
VcpD gene sequence, 82
vertical transmission, 31
Vibrio cholerae
   antibiotic resistance. *See*
      antibiotic resistance
   bacteriophages, 29–30
      and cAMP, 68–70
   diarrhea-causing mecha-
      nism, 57–68
   electron micrograph of,
      18, 68
   flagellum and fimbria, 28
   genome, 77–88
   as Gram negative bacteria,
      21, 22
   immune response, 27–29
   isolation of specimens,
      24–25
   Robert Koch's studies, 16,
      20–21
   life cycle, 113
   MCP genes, 83
   in oceans, 45–46, 86, 111
   origin of name, 19
   as prokaryote of domain
      bacteria, 25–26
   properties, 20–32

survival on body or clothing of victim, 48
virulence of, 67–76
Vibrio cholerae O1, 62, 63
Vibrio cholerae O139, 27,
   50–51, 63
vibriocidal antibodies, 106
vibrio pathogenicity island
   (VPI), 51
vibriophage, 30
Victoria (queen of
   England), 35
Victorian era, 8–10
Vienna General Hospital,
   40–41
Vietnam, 108–109
villi/villus, 67
virulence, 62, 67–76, 85
virulence factors, 47
virulence gene, 86–88, 108
virulent bacteriophage,
   29, 46
virus. *See* bacteriophage
vital force, 14
VPI (vibrio pathogenicity
   island), 51
VSP-I/II regions, 84

war, and cholera, 117
washer women's hands, 59
water containers, 101
water contamination, 53

water supply
   bioterrorism threat, 118
   Chicago epidemic, 49
   cholera bacteria survival
      in, 23–24
   clean, as best prevention,
      114
   London epidemic, 36–40
wheat ORS, 92
WHO. *See* World Health
   Organization
whole-cell injectable vaccine, 105
whole-cell oral vaccine, 109
whole-genome DNA micro-
   array, 83
World Health Organization
   (WHO)
   annual cholera case esti-
      mates, 56, 92
   climate change and dis-
      ease statistics, 117
   mortality data, 53
   ORT recommendations,
      90–91
   vaccine recommenda-
      tions, 108, 111

Zambia, 44
zone of clearing, 31
zooplankton, 43, 46, 101

About the Author

William Coleman taught microbiology to undergraduate students for 35 years. He earned a B.S. in biology at Washington College and an M.S. and Ph.D. in microbiology at the University of Chicago. He was a postdoctoral fellow at the University of Colorado Health Science Center. Upon retirement from the faculty in the College of Arts and Sciences, Department of Biology at the University of Hartford in West Hartford, Connecticut, he was promoted to professor emeritus. His research has included studies on proteins from grains toxic to eukaryotic protein synthesis systems, studies of inhibition of hormone responses by fungi, quorum sensing in *Streptococcus*, and sporulation in *Bacillus*. He served on the Bloomfield, Connecticut, Board of Education for 10 years. He was chair of the Department of Biology at the University of Hartford for three years. He was dean at Charter Oak State College, a public distance-learning institution, and is now a member of the President's Advisory Council. He is an active member of the Microbiology Education Group of the American Society for Microbiology. He has written and presented numerous articles in both basic research in biological sciences as well as those concerning improving and instilling active learning in microbiology education. He reviews and develops educational materials. He is currently a research associate at the University of Connecticut Health Center in Farmington, Connecticut. He resides in East Windsor, Connecticut.

About the Consulting Editor

Hilary Babcock, M.D., M.P.H., is an assistant professor of medicine at Washington University School of Medicine and the medical director of Occupational Health for Barnes-Jewish Hospital and St. Louis Children's Hospital. She received her undergraduate degree from Brown University and her M.D. from the University of Texas Southwestern Medical Center at Dallas. After completing her residency, chief residency, and infectious disease fellowship at Barnes-Jewish Hospital, she joined the faculty of the Infectious Disease Division. She completed an M.P.H. in Public Health from St. Louis University School of public health in 2006. She has lectured, taught, and written extensively about infectious diseases, their treatment, and their prevention. She is a member of numerous medical associations and is board certified in infectious disease. She lives in St. Louis, Missouri.